Live
God's
is Total.

H Robin

GOD
Is Talking

HINSTON ROBINSON

ISBN 978-1-64140-179-1 (Paperback)
ISBN 978-1-64258-267-3 (Hardcover)
ISBN 978-1-64140-180-7 (Digital)

Christian Faith Publishing, Inc.
296 Chestnut Street
Meadville, PA 16335
www.christianfaithpublishing.com

Printed in the United States of America

Background

Hinston M. "Rob" Robinson, the author, was raised in Georgia with his six brothers and four sisters. He received his psychology degree from Park College in Parkville, Missouri. He served in the military for over twenty years. He enlisted at eighteen years of age and was trained as a Combat Arms Infantry enlisted soldier. After his two-year enlistment was completed, he became a member of the Department of State as a member of the Foreign Service, where he served in Germany. He rejoined the Army during the Vietnam War and attended Officer Candidate School (OCS), becoming an infantry officer, and served in Vietnam. After Vietnam, he transferred to the Adjutant Generals Corps where he completed his over twenty years of military service. He was hired as a civilian working for the Army as the Personnel Proponent Advocate for Ordinance Corps officers, warrant officers, and enlisted soldiers. He is now a retired Army officer, civilian, and farmer after forty-five years of service.

Lynette K. Gough, editor and coauthor, is an adjunct English instructor at several area universities and community colleges. She is also a writing consultant with her own firm, A Great Impression, where she edits, proofreads, researches, and tutors students and adults in grammar and essay writing. Her children's books, *The Adventures of Paci* and *Treeter*, will be introduced next year.

Preface

The Beginning of My Journey

Almost drowning at a very young age started a lifetime of questions and, for me, a special understanding of my relationship over the years with my God. He has given me an introduction to his totality, and as I understand it from him, no man has the capability and capacity to fully understand it. In this introduction, I will do the best of my ability to share with you some of the thoughts he has given me over the years. I must add the free will he has given us all may have colored some of my thoughts. Now let me begin…

First, Creation: I, God, knew from the moment of your creation, and even before that, your total history. Do you not wonder why your brain does not rest? At the moment of your creation, I provided you with what many call a soul. It is my method of being in constant communication with you. It would have been simple for me to have taken full control of you, but I gave you free will to override that soul voice. This free will allows you the freedom to do some of the things I am capable of doing. These actions by your kind are sometimes judged to be good or evil by you. In fact, they are neither good nor evil in my eyes, just a reflection of my totality. This does not mean that a group of you cannot form communities and agree upon standards by which you live. You also have the capacity and the capability to punish those who do not comply with these standards. But to punish in my name or to judge in my name is beyond man's understanding of me. Punish and judge in your own name, by your own rules, and take responsibility for your actions, *but not in my name.*

Love. As you do not understand my totality, you cannot be expected to understand my total love and acceptance of you. Your brain cannot accept my totality or completeness; the wonder, doubt, dread, and a myriad of negativity crowd into your thoughts, and your faith is shattered. My love and acceptance of you are total. It does not fail or wander. It is always there for your comfort. In your darkest hour, know that I am with you, and regardless of what you may have done, my love and acceptance of you are complete and total. Let this understanding warm your days and comfort you at night, for I am always with you, and I do not condemn you. What is right and wrong? You have your ideas of right and wrong. Your ideas of right and wrong are not my ideas. Think about what happens that man has no control over: the death of a beloved child, sickness, storms, floods, even the day-to-day sun and moon rising and setting, the seasons…who controls all these things?

Man has no control over my hand. Man, on the other hand, was created by me to assist me in reflecting my totality. The kindness and love that can be shown to his fellowman is a reflection of who I am. But you must look at man's total being: his enslavement of others, wars, and the development of weapons, which can destroy whole cities, laboratories that produce killer diseases, drugs, and other destructive methods, all to kill and control. Your greed reduces whole communities to starvation and poverty. These too are only a few of man's abilities to reflect my totality. You must understand, and by your understanding of who I am, understand I control both of what you call right and wrong, and to this end, there is no good or evil in my eyes. No one is my equal. No one or nothing has this total control but me.

Judgment. Man does not have the understanding to judge my works. Your free will allows you to judge that which you do, but not in my name. If you look at all the peoples of your world, some have values that are so different from yours, so you judge them to be wrong, or even evil. But they have been given the same rights and free will you have been given. If I had not desired this reflection of my totality, I would not have given man free will. Look at the world. All things that exist are by my hand. When man judges these things I have created, he neither has the capacity of understanding nor the wisdom to judge in my name. His judgment of my works is futile. My work will stand forever; man's will fade away.

Acceptance. You are by my hand. Your acceptance by me is complete. Others may not accept you, but never fear because the one that matters accepts you. You may ask, "What does that mean?" It means that in my eyes, you are perfect. Do you think I would create someone or something that would not please me? You may make choices in your clothes, hair, or even body that others may find faulty, but I do not. Listen to that soul voice. If you stay in tune with it, you stay in tune with me. Even if you do not stay in tune with your soul voice, my acceptance of you is total.

Joy. Living with joy is my goal for each one of my creations. There are a few simple rules, but rules that are hard to follow. Rule number one: you must have total trust in me. That means everything that happens to you is by my hand and is for your benefit. Rule number two: do not worry. If you worry, you will miss out on the joy of living. You cannot change anything by worrying, so why worry? Rule number three: love yourself. By loving yourself, you can love others, and most importantly, love me. I know everything long before anything happens to you, what is going to happen, and how you will react. Place your love and trust in me. Your welfare is important to me, and I have the strength and power to look after you. Rule number four: stay in tune with your soul voice. I have provided this as one of the most important tools in keeping yourself in balance and in touch with me. The joy you will experience with this balance is beyond belief. As you learn to use your soul voice to align yourself, your joy will increase. Living with joy is living with your soul as I created it to live with me.

Change. Change has been a constant in your life since your conception. While change is constant, living with change and what it brings can, for some, be very difficult. As a young boy or girl, the changes to your body was both a joy and a period of doubt: will you be pretty or good-looking, will you be liked, all of those things that come with growing into adults. Then as the years pass, your body begins to show the stress of time. Changes are on the march. You lose some or all of your hair, your skin begins to sag and become thin, and the slightest bump will leave you with a cut or a bruise. Then your health begins to fail, and your mind is not as sharp as it once was. You forget old friends and good times. You reflect more and more on days gone by, but this change is also by my hand. Live and use this change to draw closer to me. Your bodily changes allow you a closer walk with me, a total joy. For you, these steps seem simple, but I know how difficult it is to accept and follow them.

Life. To sum up, my relationship with man is, for me, quite simple. I created you in my image; therefore, you are a reflection of who I am. This reflection was created to reflect my totality. You see, each of you, as you live out your lives, reflect who I am. From conception to what you call death, you reflect who I am. Some of you reflect what you judge to be good, while others reflect what you judge to be evil. I know your acceptance of me, being all things, is difficult for you, but for you to understand my total acceptance of you, I must reflect all ways and things that you do. I have given all of your capabilities, which, in some small way, reflect who I am, my totality. On one hand, I have placed no restriction on your abilities, but without using the building blocks I have given you, you cannot create anything new. The building blocks can be changed by you to build wonders of the world, clothe, feed, and do other things, some by your standards good and bad. Changing or using my building blocks have produced wonders, but they pale when compared to the wonders I created and provided to you. Change will come to you, but you, as with all things I have created, will not be destroyed. Death as you know it is, for me, just another change.

Change. You will change, but this change is by my design, and as I have been with you before, I will be with you after. I will always be with you. My love and acceptance of you do not change. Take comfort in my love and acceptance of you. You will always be with me, and I will always be with you. One final note from me, the author, as you read this book: in this book, I have written only those thoughts that are relevant to this book. The only two clear talks with God were when I was a young boy—once when I almost drowned and once when I fell out of a tree. It may have been a lack of oxygen to my brain, as some would have me believe, but I still hear and feel his voice and his presence in my life today. These two important occurrences started me on a road that has benefited me beyond measure and has helped me in a relationship with my God. This book is written so others who may wonder about life and that inner voice may know that at least one other person has walked down part of their road. I wish them a rewarding and joyous trip.

Introduction

God! Who Are You?

I am all the things that you have seen and the things that you have not seen and will never see. The sounds you hear are only the sounds that you are physically able to hear. I hear all the sounds from earth and the heavens, from the wind blowing through pine needles to the colliding of stars in the heavens. I feel your love, your hate, and all the emotions you have, which are also mine. I am totality. I am all things. I am complete. I am changed. Without me, there would be nothing. I am the joy that a mother feels when she holds her baby to her breast to feed it for the first time. I am also the mother who is repulsed by her newborn and takes its life. I am the father whose chest almost bursts with pride at his son's abilities on the ball field. Likewise, I am also the father who abandons his son without a thought. I am the couple who love and care for each other as I am also the couple who hates and tries to make each other as unhappy as possible.

All make these choices based upon this free will. I am he who sees and loves the things I have created. We feel the same joy in seeing the hummingbird guard its space by shooting a fake dart at its opponent. We laughed when we saw a newborn calf try out its legs for the first time. We share the first clumsy run of this calf. For you see, all the things you feel, I also feel. The things you do are part of who I am. As you reflect a part of me, I reflect all of you. In my totality, all that exists is by my hand. All the things you can conceive of are only those things you have experienced. Your time has been conceived by night as it turns to day and day to night, the seasons, and the change that occurs during these periods. These changes were conceived by me and given by my hand to you. Change is a key to understanding one part of who I am. Take the seasons, such as the joy of spring, new life, when trees put on new leaves and grow; or in the summer when the heat brings a maturation of the plants; or in the fall, a time to harvest and for plants to drop their seeds; or in the winter with the cold, the snow, and a period of dormancy. Then this cycle starts over again but with changes. The giant old oak did not make it through the winter to start another spring. The area around it will go through major periods of change in the years to come. But for many years, it has dropped several seeds, and now a number of little oak trees are beginning to grow. Some will replace the old giant oak. All of these are by my hand, just as you were conceived by my hand and grew.

When you heard your mother talking (praying) to me as she milked the cow that provided some of the food for your family, she gave thanks to me for all ten of you that were alive. She also remembered the one that died as an infant by my hand. She believed she was blessed, and so she was, by my hand. As a baby, you were totally dependent on someone to protect you, feed you, and keep you warm and clean so that you could grow and, by the way, change. In time, you became mobile. Soon you could eat food from the table like your older brothers and sisters.

Change. Then off to school you went, and then by my hand, you did not drown. Life is eventful with so many changes. Then it was time to leave home. Change. Your free will made you decide to join the Army. Big change. This was the first time, at eighteen, you had been on your own. But by this time, we had talked several times, and your buddies had not peed on you—good laugh. You have now grown old according to your understanding of time. But our talks have given you the briefest understanding of time, as time exists without a beginning or an end for me. That is my time. I share your thoughts and know what is in your mind, even though we have discussed changes, which will surely happen to you. I know the difficulty in accepting what you believe to be the final change. Remember as you walk this path, you are a part of me and cannot be destroyed. That which I have created cannot be destroyed. Changed, yes, but destroyed, no.

You are one of my creations. You have been with me always. Your time will have what you believe to be a beginning and an end. My time, not like your time, has no beginning and no end as you reflect only one aspect of who I am. You can share with others of your kind who you think I am and your relationship to me. How you are able to see me is unique. My greatness is reflected in all things. You marvel at one of my beautiful sunsets and look on in horror at the destruction of one of my floods, but both are by my hand. You question the flood. Do you question the sunset? Why do you question my work? These are both by my hand. You cannot create the beauty of the sunset, nor can you make the rain that falls that create the flood. However, by using the building blocks and the materials and tools I created and gave to you, you can change the sunset with your air pollution and channel the flood waters with your great machines that would not exist without me. These are only two examples of the many changes you can make by using the building blocks I have provided to you.

You can now fly in the sky like a bird and travel in space like the rays from the sun. You have created cities and weapons that destroy these cities in seconds. These cities have been changed in the blink of an eye, changed by you. The people's flesh burned off their bones, and others live in sickness and filth, all using material and tools I provided. You have changed winter to summer and summer to winter by interfering with the ozone layer on my earth, but my hand still controls all changes and any changes to come. You may use the material and tools I have given you, but you cannot destroy. Change! You are only one instrument of change. Changes not of your doing are those you will never see, understand, or envision. I have, however, provided you with some of the tools necessary to accept and accommodate some of these changes. Your understanding of me and my works vary widely among all of you. Some of you have the limited wisdom to understand and see the wonders of these changes by my hand. Others see the horrors of my work and judge these harshly.

You have asked, "Who are we?" You alone have been given the material, tools, and abilities to use them in expressing your free will. I have also given you the ability to use your senses to take in what I have created. Your free will, by using my materials and tools, has allowed you to become a force for change. You build homes and cities, treat and cure diseases, communicate in a flash the world over, and travel the globe and into space, to name only a few of the things I allow you to do. I will not and do not intervene.

However, do not think in the time of your history I have not heard the plans for my intervention, that I have not seen the horror that mankind can conceive and carry out against their brothers and sisters. Man has enslaved children who were taken from the arms of their fathers and mothers. Men, women, and children are made to work in mines, factories, and fields to support a lifestyle of leisure for the rich and famous, who believe they were blessed by me to enjoy the fruits of others without any effort to earn on their part. But their excesses do give rise to action. Both actions, greed, and corrective action were also by my hand. The same demand for change occurs when a nation or a people believe they have a right to exploit or enslave others, regardless of the method of enslavement or exploitation. In building your country, your founding fathers set forth principles that have allowed you to become a powerful nation.

Let us look at the changes that were made along the way. There were those who were powerful and used their positions to convince others that all men were not endowed by me to be equal. Therefore, their property could be taken by force if necessary. Those living on the land for generations could be herded like cattle and confined to reservations with very limited rights. The men who took over this land and reduced generations of people into servitude used tools I provided to take land and destroy a people. The horror of their actions still resound throughout your history.

Your nation at this time was also growing. Factories were being built in the north. Large fields cleared for crops and large plantations were being built in the south. These two sections, north and south, were building a nation. The need for labor was a problem. The north had a steady stream of poor European immigrants with manufacturing skills who settled there. The south, on the other hand, needed but did not have a large source of cheap labor. The foundation of a disaster was about to be laid.

Your founding fathers again allowed mankind to be divided into a superior race and one to be subjected or enslaved. The slave ships from Africa, Europe, and South America came with a steady stream of enslaved labor. These men, women, and children were sold on the auction block to the highest bidder without regard of their commitment to one another then or in the future. Any man could buy a slave, and the character of these men and the use of these human beings by him was of no concern to the system of government he helped create that was supposed to represent everyone. The enslaved men, women, and children became property to be sold and traded without any regard for them as human beings. If you listen, you can still hear the cries of siblings, mothers, fathers, all crying for their losses. The beatings left scars on almost every part of some of the slaves' bodies, including the dog bites from the slaves being hunted. I watched and knew of your actions, but I did not intervene. Your free will was at work.

This is part of who you are, your history. A few men and women saw the horror of this system, and change was in the wind. This is also who you are. The price to be paid was the death and wounded bodies of thousands of men and young boys and the destruction of cities and homes throughout your country. Maybe this is a high price to be paid for free will. But the price will be paid time and time again, now and in the future.

Free men and women? Yet some men's ability and their need to control and enslave others go on. The creation of the company or country store was a unique system used by factories and landowners to enslave and control working free men, women, and children before and after the Civil War. This system is still used today. In the "good old days," with little or no transportation, the one company or country store was an entrapment out of necessity for some people with limited means. You worked, and at some time, normally payday or in the fall when the crops were harvested, you paid the store and always lacked a little to pay off your bill. If the storeowner did not own the coal mine, factory, or farm on which you lived, one of his friends or a relative did. The law was no help if a dispute arose. The law was the store's enforcer.

The explosion of men entering World War II and women entering the workforce to make up for men at war and the rise of labor unions helped solve some of the problems. However, men's and women's greed still enslave others, and the horror of their enslavement does not go unnoticed by me. From the moment of your conception, you have lived with change, all in preparation for you to accept change. As you grew, your reliance on others changed. Some of you grew less reliant on others, but all of you retain a degree of reliance on me. Some of you have developed a strong reliance on your concept of self, while others have tried to believe that I do not exist. By expressing their free will, a person will take one path, and the other will choose a different path.

Both are reflective of who I am. One is not more correct than the other, but both fulfill my plan. At any time, I could change the horrors caused by your greed and your belief in self-importance, but think: if I controlled your free will, you would be no different than all the other creatures and everything else I have created and controlled. I would not need you. You are allowed to express your free will in all aspects of life, such as greed for material wealth, lust for others, property, feeling of superiority, enslavement, killing, and many other horrors, but you are also allowed to express your freewill by loving, caring, feeling, and becoming a person of action. I allow you all these attributes to reflect my totality. That is who you are, and that is your purpose: to reflect me and my totality.

Chapter 1

This is a life story of growing up and talking to God.

I grew up in a large family often with just two year's difference in most of our ages. Until I was seven or eight, my life had been just like all the other kids in our farming community. In my family, all of us were expected to behave and do our fair share of the house and farmwork. I must admit I was not the best farmhand in our family. My younger sister and the sister just older than me could pick more cotton. The older sister was the best chopper of cotton in the family and probably in the county. She never let the rest of us forget how good she was. What a pain in the behind. My older brother by just two years could plow and run the planters like a pro, and he was not intimidated by the mules. The mules could sense my fear, according to my dad, and that was the reason that they did not gee-haw or mind and follow my commands, like they did for my brother. Again, my brother let me know what a wimp I was for not letting the mules know who the boss was. Big brother: pain in the behind too. I still think the mules knew I did not to work, and so neither did they.

Our lives consisted, most of the time, of going to school, riding the bus home, and changing out of our "school clothes" into work clothes, which were faded from being washed in lye soap because my mother believed in keeping us clean and from being handed down from an older brother or sister. My mother also kept our clothes patched because she did not like to see us raggedy. So off came school clothes and shoes, and field clothes went on, and to the fields we went day after day. In the summertime, I can still feel the hot plowed dirt going between my toes. What a joy, what a feeling. There was wood to be cut for the cookstove, summer and winter, and the only heated room in the house that had an open fireplace was the room we stayed in until bedtime in the winter. The rest of the house was as cold as the outdoors, and going outside to relieve ourselves was no joy. Thank goodness for the Sears & Roebuck catalog and the Atlanta Constitution. They were our source of wiping paper. If you grabbed a page of the Atlanta newspaper, you had better hope that our dad had read it. If not, you were in for trouble. The last year's old Sears & Roebuck catalog was also our wiping paper at school. I now wonder if Sears & Roebuck knew their "wish book" had been a godsend for another purpose. It sure beat an oak leaf. When I look back at these times, they were filled with a feeling of belonging, safety, and joy, but some of the good old days were not so good or, at least, enjoyable.

Not much changed in our daily routine, and when something did come up, you can imagine the excitement among us all. When we got invited to go to our aunt and uncle's new lake for a picnic and a day of fun, we could hardly control ourselves. On that eventful day, we all loaded on our father's truck, and away we went. Along the way, we picked up some other people who had also been invited. Transportation in those days was a shortage. You shared with your neighbors.

Everything was going great. My aunt and uncle's family and some other families had been invited, and everyone had brought something good to eat. It was a good crowd. The lake was warm, and the adults as well as the kids were having a ball. At the time, I could dog paddle and stay afloat, but I could not swim. The most fun was riding on some logs left in the lake. I was on one of these logs and kicking with my legs and feet and paddling with my hands when the log spun, and I went underwater like a rock. I remember thinking, *This is it. I'm going to die.* I was not afraid. I accepted it and was at peace. I think a kid at that age probably does not know enough about life to be afraid of dying.

During this period of peace, a voice said, *Not yet.* The husband of one of my aunt and uncle's daughters, my older cousin's husband, had seen me bobbing up and down, and he jumped in and pulled me out. On the bank, I asked him why he said, "Not yet."

He looked at me kind of funny and said, "I didn't." The rest of the day was no fun for me. I sat alone in the sun. After what seemed like hours, Mom and Dad rounded up all of us kids, along with the others, to take us home. Going home on the back of the truck, my older brother, Plowboy, and my sisters kept saying how I spoiled their day. One of them said, "At least, you could have drowned, and if we were lucky, the funeral would be on a workday."

Plowboy said, "Now we will just have to go back to work and have no place to go, shithead." My oldest brother on the trip said, "You can bet your last dollar our uncle will never allow us to be invited back to his lake." He was right.

In a few days, life was back to normal. It was summer, no school, just working and trying to stay hidden to get out of work and out of the way. That is not easy as you might think, with a number of brothers and sisters wanting to rat you out. Even with what went on, time seemed to pass so slowly, but before we knew it, we were back in school with our new Sears & Roebuck clothes. All of the kids dressed alike because nearly every parent ordered from Sears & Roebuck. To have something not ordered from Sears & Roebuck was a rarity, and it gave you a showoff status among friends at school. Mom did make some of our boy's shirts and the girl's dresses. She was a good seamstress, and those clothes gave us some individuality and limited bragging rights.

Life went on for a few years without a hitch. Then one Sunday, it happened. A group of us boys were playing in the woods. Someone suggested we go swing out on some trees. My older brother, Plowboy, said, "I know where some good ones are." Like a bunch of wild things, off through the woods we went. He was right. There was a grove of hickory and poplar trees. The hickory trees were just right for swing-ing out. We were all having a ball. Then someone said, "Look at that big one. I bet no one will swing out of it." Everyone was daring each other to climb to the top and swing out. After being called chicken, with a lot of ribbing and getting no nays, I gave in. Up the tree I went with all of them cheering me on.

When I got where I could grasp near the top, my brother, Plowboy, said, "Hey, shithead, that's not a hickory. That's a poplar, and it will break off when you swing out." I thought he was just envious of the attention I was getting. By this time, with all the cheering and hollering, I could not back down. I was going to do it. I grabbed as close to the top as possible, put my bare feet against the tree, and leaned back. The loud pop I heard was the top breaking off. The top of the tree and I hit the ground. I couldn't move or speak. All I could do was listen. "Is he dead?" a boy asked.

Another one said, "I think so. What are we going to do?" Another boy said, "I don't know, but we are in a lot of doo-doo." I heard another voice that said, "I remember when Grandmaw brought Grandpaw back from the dead. When we told Grandmaw that Grandpaw was dead, she said, 'Show me.' Me and my brother took her where Grandpaw was propped up against a big old oak tree by the spring we used for water. Grandmaw said, 'You want to see a dead man walk and holler?' Of course, my brother and I wanted to see. Grandmaw went to the spring with the bucket she had carried with her and got a full bucket of cold spring water. She told us to stand back, and she threw it on Grandpaw. Grandpaw jumped up with a loud holler, and after a cold stare, he asked, 'Why did you do that, old woman?' She said, 'That's what you get when you hit the sauce too heavy.'"

Another voice said, "How does that story help us?" Another young boy said, "We could pull him to that tree and prop him up. That might help." Another voice said, "We don't have any water to pour on him, though." Then another voice said, "We could all pee on him. That might work." While I could hear those voices and what they were planning, I could do nothing. I could not move. They pulled me over to the tree, and while they were deciding what to do, one of them said, "If we pee on him, and he's all wet when they find him dead, we will be in more deep trouble. Let's just leave him here and let them find him when he doesn't show up for supper."

They all agreed, and off they went, whooping and hollering, without a care in the world. Then the feeling I had when I almost drowned came back, but this time it was somewhat different. It was like someone was holding me, all warm and cuddly, full of merriment and laughter. In a clear voice, I heard, *Not yet*, again.

This time, I asked, "Who are you?"

The answer was clear: *God.*

I said, "God does not talk to us."

The voice said, *How do you know what I can do?*

I said to him, "I'm not going to tell anyone I heard you. They will think I'm nuts."

God said, *You may be right, but you are free to do as you wish. My gift is free will.*

Then I opened my eyes, and I began to laugh. "Pee on him!" I felt the humor of the situation. It was a good day for me. What follows in this book are several conversations over seventy years grouped together concerning subjects that are not related to time. The closeness and the feeling of someone or something outside of myself was confusing for a nine-year-old. The two events above were the strongest and clearest memories, but they formed the foundation for listening to God. What follows is my reconciliation of his literal and figurative guidance in my life. The most difficult part is knowing what he wants and what you want. I must admit what I wanted ruled the day too many times.

Chapter 2

"God, do you play a part in all our lives?" This started a conversation that has been ongoing for a very long time. "I am God!" he said. Then he asked, "Who are you?"

My answer, as I recall, was, "I am just a kid who likes to play with his friends, walk in the woods, play with the farm animals, do chores I hate, and who works, eats, and sleeps in a warm bed with a family who keeps me safe, sound, and loved."

"Do you think that is all you are?"

I did not know. That was the end of the conversation for that day. However, from that day forward, I could feel a presence. He was always with me and in my mind, keeping me almost on track with my values. I was just beginning to understand free will. The days and years that follow have been lived by his grace and getting me back on track after I used my free will out of balance with who I am.

Starting out in life is very simple for a lot of kids...not too much to think about, just having as much fun as you can doing the things that you like that are exciting and bring joy and fun into your life. At this time, I thought all kids had good parents, friends, and support. Boy, was I stupid.

I'm not sure adults, or even parents, know how much influence they have in shaping a child's future and our thoughts, such as my mother's talks with God as she milked and my father's stern show of approval or disapproval. An example: one day, for some reason, I was walking down the sidewalk with my father in this small town near where we lived. We were side by side, and I was big-timing it to be with him. Ahead of us was this black lady with her little boy, who was my size, walking toward us. I was going to stand my ground. The lady pulled her son behind her, and as we came closer, she was about to give me her side of the sidewalk when I felt a jerk and a strong arm putting me behind my father.

As she passed, she looked at my father and said, "God bless you, sir."

My father said, "The same to you and your son." The message was loud and clear to me.

Respect has no age or color restriction. Over the years, building on this experience, I have learned you can only respect others to the extent you have respect for yourself. His voice again in my head said, *Get ready for change.* These short alerts or messages became common.

The major turning point for a kid is the beginning of adulthood, which started for me at about twelve or thirteen. My body was changing. I was developing muscles I never had, and hair was growing on my face and around "it." The hair I could deal with, but "it" was a problem. Of course, all my buddies were having the same problem. Some of them claimed to know all about what was happening. The information they shared along those lines was that if you played with "it," you would go blind or die or it would fall off and all kinds of other things, and worst of all, God would punish you. We all thought we knew someone God had punished for using "it." To make matters worse, some of that information was provided by "well-meaning" adults, which meant it had to be true. Adults do not lie. Adjusting to "it" was a major crisis for some of us kids or, if you prefer, young adults. In the fifties, sex education was not a subject to be taught in schools or in our homes. You were on your own to figure it out. Today's kids probably know more than grownups did back when I was a teenager. We were all dumb.

My "it" was not falling off. I was not going blind, and as far as I could tell, I was not dying. I tried my best not to touch or play with it: impossible. The only problem I could tell was sometimes waking up with a handful of goo with the sheets a little messed up. I know

23

my mother, who washed the sheets, must have noticed. No information came from her on the nature of my problem. I needed help.

"God! What is wrong with me?" Then the questions and comments began.

"Why do you think something is wrong with you?"

"You know what my buddies and a few adults, the ones who are talking, are saying about the consequences of playing with *it*, and sometimes it just does its own thing."

"I know. This is the first major change in your life that you have noticed so much. There will be many more. Use them to learn and grow. But you want help with this one now. First, do you think I would give you something and then punish, or even kill, you for using it? Of course not. You kids do not know, and even some of the adults know about as little as you do. The gift of *it* and the pleasure it can bring was given to both you and again, to your surprise, to girls. I know that at your age, for both girls and boys, it can be difficult. As all things given to you, there come responsibilities. You have the free will to use them as tools to enhance your life and, in the future, your partner's life. Rejoice now and enjoy the gift in accordance with your value system. You are not going blind, *it* won't fall off, and you will not die." *Thank God*, I thought.

And with those assurances, I went back to being a carefree teenager. We chased girls, they chased us, and it was a good time for all, falling in and out of "love" daily. A few of my buddies by this age, from about thirteen to sixteen years old, talked about "loose girls" or girls who were "putting out" and how good it had been with them. I had heard adults use the word *whore* to describe loose women who "put out," but my buddies were talking about girls who were our friends. Something was wrong. Questions started going off in my mind: What about my buddies? Were they not putting out? What do you call them? Don't they share responsibility for the stigma being leveled at the girls?

I decided to ask my father. It took all of my courage I had to ask him the question about boys' responsibilities. He looked at me for a long while and said, "Boys are different. They can't have babies." As dumb as I was, I knew that. Looking at my father, I knew that was the end of that conversation. Like most of my buddies, you see, I had both brothers and sisters. He was the father to both. At that time, even though I knew there was one, I did not understand the social stigma attached to a girl who got pregnant but was not married or had to marry because she was pregnant. After the boy-buddy question to my father, in my mid-teens, I was allowed to sit at the table while my parents and other adults discussed this subject. It was the beginning of my education, even though I had not connected the discussion and my responsibility at the time and using "it" in line with my values and also those of my family. From the conversations, I learned that some families did not or would not require their sons to accept their responsibilities to the girl or to their baby. In their minds, it was the girl's fault. She was alone to take full responsibility, and in some cases, even her family disowned her. Other families required what was called shotgun weddings, while others rejoiced, and even had big weddings, just like nothing had happened but a blessed event. For my family, my father left no doubt as to accepting responsibility: both girls and boys would be held equally responsible. The family would accept responsibility and try to work out the best arrangement for the boy, the girl, and the two families. If this were not possible, our family would take full responsibility in line with the wishes of the boy and the girl. End of discussion. But regardless, at the time, the girl always received most of the blame for what happened, and this blame came from both men and women.

The days of my parents providing food, clothing, and a caring home was coming to an end. The changes God had spoken to me about were looming. In May, I would graduate from high school, and my eighteenth birthday was the first part of June. What was I going to do? My other brothers had all served in the military. That was an option. I did not have the money to go to college, and while my parents would have borrowed money for me, I did not want to go down that road. I did not know about scholarship funds, and no one in our high school discussed funding sources. I'm not sure they even knew. Too bad. So the military was looking better and better. The only question I had was, what if I don't like it? I knew people who did not like it but made it through the two-year draft. So, I decided to go to the local draft board and volunteer.

They were glad to help out, which meant they did not have to select someone else that month. They had to meet their quota. I was drafted on 13 July 1956, and I reported to the Army induction center in Atlanta, Georgia. The fun was about to begin. For a boy, a young adult, from rural Georgia in the fifties, the assault on my privacy was just short of overwhelming. Some of the guys were even crying and wanting to go home. It was quite a shock. Even swimming in the nude with my buddies at the old swimming hole and the locker room before and after school sports had not prepared me for running around with over a hundred-plus naked men or boys of all colors and shapes.

Instructions: bend over, turn your head and cough, touch your toes, lean over the table, "spread 'em," and several other moves I had never made, or had even heard of. More instructions: get in line, both arms down by your sides, do not move as both arms were being assaulted with one shot after another. The day was over. We had been poked in every part of our bodies, and our arms were sore and bleeding from so many shots. You see, the instructions not to move your arms was good advice. The air guns they were using to give shots would leave a nice little circular cut if you moved. They did not say the cut would occur if the guy giving you the shot moved, so most of us ended up with several small cuts, which hurt like hell. The next day, which was draw clothes day, started early with our sore arms. The first issue was a large canvas green bag or duffel bag to put in everything you were issued. Your new army clothing, uniforms, socks, underwear, snot rags, their name for handkerchiefs, and ties were being thrown at you with the speed and efficiency of an assembly line that Henry Ford would have been proud of. The end of the line was for getting boots. Instructions: walk up to the counter and holler out the size of shoes you wear. To my surprise, some guys did not know what size of shoes they wore. If this happened, a soldier behind the counter would say, "Hold up your feet." He would then say, "Looks like a pair of tens would fit." Then he would holler, "Throw me a pair of tens," and on we went. By the end of the line, the duffel bag was packed, and our boots and low quarters or dress shoes hung around our necks.

The next step was to find you a table and dump all your stuff out. The sergeant, or SGT, a rank below lieutenant and who is not an officer but is in charge of many different functions in the Army, told us what to do. "Now this is a clothing issue form," he said. "It lists everything you are supposed to have. We will now check off each item. If you are missing an item, sound off like you got a pair. Okay, let's start," he said, holding up an item. "If you have two pairs of these, mark them off and throw them into your duffel bag. Let me warn you again, if you don't have what I hold up in the numbers when I say 'sound off,' after we complete this process, you will sign the clothing issue form, and you will buy any future shortages. Got it?"

"Yes, Sergeant." We were learning.

"If the boots and low quarters don't fit, don't worry. They are the only items that you can exchange when you get to your basic combat training location. Got it?"

Again, we said, "Yes, Sergeant."

"Sign the form! Get out of my sight, you lowlife! I've had a bad day." He did not ask and did not seem to care about our day. It was the end of that processing day. We took all of our new belongings back to our bunks and passed out. It had been a long day for us too.

The next two days were for testing to make sure we were trainable and what training was in the Army's best interest, in other words, what the Army needed. So, it was determined that most of us draftees were best suited for the infantry. By the end of the week, we were ready to be shipped to our new basic training site. By this time, we were starting to develop new friends.

Change! The ability to form relationships with people under-going similar events was remarkable to me because up to this point, I had known my friends for years. God's message! "Relax and enjoy your friends and experiences and learn from them. This is a period of learning, accepting responsibility, and growing up. During this period, you will build a foundation that you, your family, friends, others, and I have started. To answer your question, you are right! I am always by your side." That was a question on my mind. We loaded on buses and were on our way to Fort Jackson, South Carolina, which is where we all expected to attend Basic Combat Training or BCT. Some of the guys on the bus had never been out of the county in which they were born and grew up. Thanks to my family, mostly older brothers and sisters, I had been to Atlanta and out of state to Mobile, Alabama, and to other places several times. Therefore, I was a world traveler to some of the guys. In the limelight, I pretended to know more than I did, but it was fun being important for a while.

We arrived late at night. Why the Army always planned for you to arrive late at night, I never figured out. We arrived late, ate chow or had a meal, made up our bed, slept for two to three hours, and then we were up for breakfast to start another day. To almost everyone's surprise, the breakfast was not bad, and you got all you wanted, except if you took it, you had to eat it. We learned that was rule number one when eating in an Army dining facility or mess hall. Hurry up and eat, more prodding, and all kinds of other "detail" or what the army calls regular "work." The idea was to keep us busy.

While all this was going on, we had more testing, and then we received orders to our BCT site. What a surprise—all of the draftees received orders to go to Fort Knox, Kentucky. I was the only eigh-teen-year-old in the group. All the other draftees were in their twen-ties, and a large number of them had college degrees. Boy! What an education an eighteen-year-old with only a high school education was in for. In all fairness, I became like a younger brother to most of them.

When we arrived at Fort Knox, Kentucky, again late at night, we were assigned to the Fourth Platoon or PLT. One of our new platoon sergeants was there to show us our barracks. To our surprise, the beds were made up, and name tags hung from each bed. The PLT sergeant or SGT said, "Find the bunk (or bed) with your name on it, sign the form for your bedding, which I will collect, and this is your home for the next eight weeks." We did as we were told. It took about an hour. The PLT sergeant then instructed us that the lights would go out in ten minutes. "So be in your bunk. It's going to be a busy day tomorrow. Good night, ladies." Because our platoon was made up of more older guys than the other three platoons, we were always leading the pack in training. I do not think any of the other soldiers in the other platoons knew that I was the same age as they were but only that I had been drafted. I am glad they did not know and that they were giving me a lot of brotherly advice. Some of the key advice was, "Get a college degree." This advice came from guys who had degrees and those who did not. They all agreed it did not matter too much what subject, just get the degree, which they said would open doors that would never open without the degree. Again, more advice!

Marry a rich girl, total agreement, because money is very nice to have, and it can make up for a lot of things: nagging, looks, bad temper, in-laws, outlaws, and most importantly, bad sex. With that one, they would all have a good laugh and agree it took a lot of money to make up for that one. Then the discussion was centered on how much money. No amount was ever agreed upon.

I asked the guy who was my best soldier buddy out of the group and whom I trusted the most what they were talking about when they said "bad sex." He was a college graduate and had started to get his master's degree in mathematics when he was drafted. He was our "smart guy" and was looked up to by the whole platoon. He looked at me kind of funny with the same stare my father had given me years earlier. I was hoping I would get a better answer. Boy, did I get a better answer. He asked me point-blank if I had ever had intercourse. Before I could answer, he answered for me, "I thought not. Let's go over to the snack bar." The snack bar was a place you buy beer and short-order food, such as hamburgers, french fries, etc. He did not ask anyone else to go with us. I was glad. This conversation was too personal to share with just anyone.

When we got to the snack bar, he ordered us two beers, which all the real beer drinkers said was like water, and we sat down to have a drink. I hated beer and still do, but I was not about to jeopardize the informational meeting I was about to hear. He looked again at me and said, "This stays between you and me, okay?" Of course, I said, "Okay."

He started by telling me that when he was almost twenty, he had married a beautiful girl, and both of them had been very much in love, or so they thought. It turned out that the only thing they had in common was "good sex." For months, they tried to figure out what was wrong. They complained to each other, their friends, their family, and even went to a marriage counselor, who was also their minister. Even with this help and insight, they both knew that they needed to part ways. The divorce was friendly, and he said they were still good friends. After this story, he looked straight into my eyes and said, "'Good sex-bad sex' does not hold a relationship together. Do you get the point?" I did because I realized that was what God had told me years before. But I wanted to hear more about good sex, or even bad sex. So I said, "Tell me about sex." He looked at the snack bar clock and said, "Later. If we don't want to go on detail forever, we had better not miss bed check." So off we went at a run to get into bed before lights out and bed check. We made it. Later that night, and before I went to sleep, I thought about the conversations I had with God and how I was changing into adulthood. My buddy had just shared with me a part of his life for my benefit and promised to share more. At this point in my life, I did not think I had ever shared my life or thoughts with anyone. I knew for sure I had not shared them with the goal of helping someone. *Is this something you do as an adult?* I thought. A loud "Yes!" came into my mind.

Breakfast came early that morning. We were going to the bivouac area for four days. We would pitch our tents and then march to the rifle range where we would qualify with our assigned weapons, which at that time was a heavy M1 rifle. My tent buddy was also a college graduate who talked little, and when he could, he slept. The rest of the platoon called him Rip Van Winkle. After the bivouac for two days, I understood why. Our PLT had the combined highest score of any PLT who had ever received BCT at Fort Knox, Kentucky, at that time. We also had the largest number of soldiers qualifying as experts. I did not shoot expert but qualified as a marksman. I was happy. The way the PLT had performed made the cadre and the company commander very proud. Some of the more experienced guys said this gave them bragging rights at the officers' club for officers and NCOs or noncommissioned officers' club for senior enlisted soldiers. The question was, what do we get? The answer came when we got back to our barracks, and everything was cleaned and stored for the next training cycle. The company commander came out to address the company. He said how proud he was with our accomplishment and thanked the cadre for all their hard work. He then announced the awards for the outstanding soldiering at the bivouac and the rifle range. All soldiers firing expert, regardless of PLT assignment, would be given an overnight pass Saturday night. The yells were loud for all of us because we were proud of our buddies, regardless of which platoon they were assigned. The commander again held up his hand, and a silence fell over the company. "Now," he said, "I want to recognize the contribution of one PLT in particular. This PLT has achieved more recognition than any other PLT since I have been a commander. Those soldiers assigned to the fourth PLT will have post privileges starting at eight hundred hours Saturday and going until seventeen hundred hours Sunday." Again we gave a loud roar of approval. His hand went up, and his parting words were, "Don't screw it up." No one screwed it up.

In just a few days, we would graduate from basic training and ship out to our Advanced Individual Training or AIT sites. The soldiers who had enlisted for three or more years knew where they were going, but all the draftees were still in the dark. Two days before graduation, an airborne recruiting team came from Fort Bragg, North

Carolina. Those soldiers who had enlisted for a Military Occupation Specialist (MOS) were told if the 82nd Airborne Division needed their MOS, they would keep their MOS and receive airborne training as a bonus. Soldiers with MOS's that the division did not need could waive their original MOS contract and go airborne with the division selecting the training, which was the basics for your new MOS. They did not say it would be infantry, but that was what most of them were assigned. The draftees could choose airborne training, and the division would determine their MOS's, again mostly infantry.

This recruiting team was so sharp, and their uniforms and boots made them stand out like some ninja warrior. Who wouldn't want to belong to a team of professionals like them? Within my group, I heard a few comments like, "What a lot of s——t." After talking to the group, we were talked to individually by the recruiter, with no time to check with my buddies as to see what they were going to do. After the interview was over, the recruiter asked, "Are you good enough to join the best?" I was signing the volunteer statement before I knew it. I walked out with my chest full of air. I was going to be the best airborne infantryman.

As I was coming out from my interview, my best buddy was coming out from his interview next door. He said, "What a bunch of shit." I looked at him and asked what he meant. He looked at me and said, "You didn't sign that volunteer statement, did you?"

"Yes!"

The next several days went by so fast it seemed like we were in some kind of time warp. My buddy never badmouthed my decision. He said, "Maybe airborne training will be good for you, and you will enjoy it. By the way, if you don't like airborne, you can always withdraw your volunteer statement and get out."

I said, "Won't that be quitting?"

He said, "Always have the courage to walk away."

Yeah. "You were going to tell me more about 'good sex and bad sex,'" I said.

He looked at me again with that older brother look and said, "I don't think you will have a hard time figuring it out. Just remember, it takes two to tango." I kind of understood.

The next day, we received orders. I was going to Fort Bragg, North Carolina, for airborne infantry training. My buddy was staying at Fort Knox, Kentucky, would receive infantry training, and would become a member of the training cadre at Fort Knox. He would be one of the best. The Army got it right. Departure day! We said our good-byes, and all promised to keep in touch, which never happened. Then we were on buses, planes, or some, like my best buddy, were left standing around; he would leave later. It was hard to be broken up from the group that had become a large family. It was especially hard to say good-bye to my "best buddy," but life goes on.

A loud "Change!" came into my conscious mind. I knew this was coming from God, just a reminder of what he had told me years before. We loaded the bus for the long ride to Fort Bragg. We would be arriving late at night, always the Army way. Same routine at Fort Jackson, not like Fort Knox: draw bedding, run to assigned bunks, make up the bed, fill out the name tag for the bed, sign a form for bedding, and then sleep for three hours if you were lucky. Breakfast again: a pleasant experience, not bad. That morning, you had a choice of eggs, bacon, cereal, milk, apple or orange juice, and what was and is still my favorite, cream of beef. We called it SOS, Shit on Shingles. It was made with dried beef or hamburger meat with just enough flour and milk to make a beef gravy. It was then spooned over toast or biscuits. If they were going to feed us like this, maybe I made the right decision of joining the best airborne infantry.

Chapter 3

The infantry training at Fort Bragg, North Carolina, did not stop except when you were in bed and asleep. You never stopped running: run to mail call, run to chow or to eat, run to physical training or PT, run to formation, run, run, and then run some more. We 120- to 150-pound weaklings were developing muscles on our bodies that any mother or father would be proud of. We had been in infantry training for seven weeks. We would graduate in the eighth week and go to Airborne School. We were all ready to go. Airborne training started on Monday with a bang. The cadre gave us hell, called us all kinds of names, and predicted that none of us would make it through their school. We were not fit to be airborne. The challenge was on. I was back with my age group with no college graduates, just us eighteen- and nineteen-year-olds who were going to show them, the cadre, what we were made of.

The first week went off without a hitch for me. The second week was tower (wooden structure) training, and that was where I picked up the name Flying Robbie. The towers were about fifty feet high. For me, they appeared to be two miles high. They said I was the only "shithead" that would stand in the door, be given the command, "Prepare to jump! Jump!" by the training cadre, and leave the door, and the first thing they knew, I was back in the tower. After a few days of trying to jump from the tower and safely slide down the guidewire to the ground, I managed to get out a few times. I was a master at kissing the ground at the end of the slide. I could beat anyone getting out of the harness, the webbing around your body, and making a perfect landing. I was so glad to be on the ground and to not have messed up my pants. I was okay. But one day, the senior trainer pulled me out of formation and said, "Let's talk."

I knew something was up because he was never this nice. He said, "I see the effort you are putting into training, but I think you have a problem with heights, and we can't fix that here. I must consider your safety as well as the safety of the other trainees and the cadre. I will recommend that you be dropped from training without prejudice, and if you want to try again someday, you can be selected." I started to beg, but he held up his hand and said, "Be at ease," which means "no talking." "I know," he continued, "how much you want to be airborne, but it is not going to happen now." Then he said, "Report to the first sergeant." (First sergeants are above master sergeants and below sergeant majors.) I remembered my best buddy's advice in BCT: "Don't be afraid to walk away." I had to walk away; I was afraid of heights.

My head hung low as I ran to the company orderly room to report to the first sergeant. I knocked on the screen door, and a loud voice said, "Come in. What do you want?"

"The senior trainer told me to report to you, First Sergeant."

"You must be Robinson."

"Yes, First Sergeant."

"Good. Can you type?"

"Yes, First Sergeant."

"Good. My sorry company clerk is on sick call, and these reports have to be typed and out of here by noon. Get on with it." The company clerk had penciled in the information needed to fill out the forms, so I sat down and typed out all the reports plus a couple of drafted letters the company clerk had left to be typed. When I finished, I handed them to the first sergeant. He looked them over and said, "Okay, from now on, you report here every day." Then he said, "Go move all of your gear (personal items) out of your barracks and into the permanent party barracks. Just find an empty bunk and claim it. If anyone dares give you a hard time, just tell them you work for me, and if they have a problem with that, tell them to come and see me. Before you go, type up your post pass and let me sign it." I did as I was told.

The next morning, I reported to the first sergeant. He introduced me to the company clerk and said to him, "This is the soldier who saved your behind. The battalion operations sergeant called and said our reports were correct and on time. Good job." I then told the first sergeant that all I did was type what his company clerk had already filled out. "Fine! Now you two get to work, and John, show Robbie the ropes." John was the company clerk or office assistant.

Then John said, "Get your hat. We're going to battalion and then to post headquarters to pick up and deliver reports and pick up supplies." As we went out the door, I started to run, and John started laughing. "You don't have to run anymore."

"Are you sure?" I said.

"I'm sure. Let's go." John turned to me and said, "Thanks for telling the first sergeant I had all those reports filled out and not just typed. We will make a good team." I had lucked out by giving John his credit. That night, as I lay awake in my bed, thinking about how badly I wanted to be airborne, a voice—his voice—said loud and clear, *You were made with a fear of heights. You have other fears, some you will overcome, some you will not. Learn from them and always have the courage to walk away. Your free will carries responsibilities and rewards. Never fear about making a decision. Your decisions are my decisions, and no man has been given the wisdom or authority to judge my decisions. How do you feel about your decision to give John credit for his work?*

"I did not know that you were there."

"I am always there. Now, how do you feel?" I had to admit I felt good about what I had done.

"You have learned two important lessons in a short time. Do not forget them. Build on them, and in time, you will realize how close you are to me."

John and I worked well together, and in two weeks, we had the best orderly room operation in the battalion according to the first sergeant, and even the company commander.

The battalion commander, who is higher in rank than the company commander, had congratulated him on getting his report in on time and correctly. The third week was kind of sad for me: my airborne class graduated and were being assigned to different airborne units on Fort Bragg. For me, that day would not come. The company was getting ready for its annual inspection. That is when the higher headquarters' staff check the total command operations. Failing one of these inspections causes everyone a lot of grief. Hours upon hours are spent in preparation for this inspection. John and I went over the company administrative functions and corrected the slightest thing that could be called an error. Some of the other sections in the company did not have the clerical support that the first sergeant had, so he asked us, or told us, to help the training office get their records straight, go and check supply, and then make sure their records were up to standards. "Okay! Get on with it!" He ordered.

John and I went to the training section first, and the voice said, "Remember, we asked the training clerk if we could help out." John said, "I know you have a lot more records to keep straight than Rob and I do in the orderly room, so if we can help, just let us know."

I said, "You will have to show us how and what to check for." He looked at us and said, "You guys really want to help? Thanks." He showed us what we needed to do to make sure the forms were all completed and correct. By two o'clock on a twenty-four-hour clock, we had checked and rechecked all the training records. One of the last training records was mine. The senior trainer had kept his promise, and in the remarks section, he had stated that Private Robinson was released from airborne training without prejudice. He even made a comment about my nickname Flying Robbie." After explaining to John and Harry, the training office clerk, what he was talking about, the three of us had a good laugh, and off we went to hit the hay or go to sleep. The next day at breakfast, we asked Harry if he thought Smith, the supply clerk, needed any help. Harry said, "He was up most of the night working on the supply records, so let's go ask him."

We all went to the supply room, and there was Smith with records all over the place.

"Same routine, John." I realized he was a master at helping people without creating offense. Harry picked up on my comment and said to Smith, "If you will show us how and if it will speed up what you have got to do, we are here."

Smith said, "Boy, could I use your help." He showed us how the issue forms, inventory, and on-hand supplies had to match. It sounded simple, but with a graduation of one-hundred-plus soldiers leaving and just day-to-day operations, it was not simple. But when we got the hang of it, the four of us were getting the pieces to fit together. We missed lunch, and by the time evening chow was ready, we were starved, so we headed for the chow hall. On the way, we met the first sergeant, the senior trainer, and the supply sergeant. The first sergeant asked us how everything was coming along.

John spoke up and said, "We are working on it."

The senior trainer spoke up and said, "I looked at the training records. To me, they look good to go."

Smith said, "We are working on the supply records. They were a mess. We should have them ready by tomorrow if we can all keep working on them."

The first sergeant said, "This is a team effort. The three of you can stay together until our company records are straight. If anyone has a problem with that, tell them to see me." If you know anything about the Army, *no one* has a problem with what the first sergeant says or wants done. That includes the officers too.

When we got to the chow hall and were eating, Harry said, "Why did you say we would be finished tomorrow? We could finish today."

Smith laughed and said, "We need a break." We all agreed and had a good laugh. "It also gives us time to recheck everything before the inspection." We finished up just like Henry said, by 20:00 hours, and agreed that we would meet the next day for a final check of our work. After that check, the inspection would start the following day and generally last for two to three days. I had never been part of an annual inspection. All of this was new to me.

The soldiers living in the barracks displayed their equipment to include assigned weapons, which lay near their bunk area. The off-post soldiers brought their equipment and clothes and were assigned different places in the company for their equipment to be inspected. By the time the inspection started, everyone was in a low/high hover. The battalion commander, a lieutenant colonel, inspected our barracks, and as he was inspecting my area, he asked me, "Have you ever been to Louisiana?"

I said, "No, sir."

"Good state. That's where I'm from. You will enjoy Fort Polk. Fort Polk has just reopened with a new mission." He looked at me again and said, "Your equipment is being maintained like an airborne soldier. Good luck in your new assignment."

I kept my mouth shut except to say, "Thank you, sir," because the first sergeant had given me the signal to keep a zipper on it. I did. The inspection lasted two and a half days, and then it was over. The results would be announced the next day by our company commander. The next morning, one hour early, the company was roused out of bed and told the company formation would be at four thirty to announce the results of the inspection. The rumor mill was in high gear—we had failed, and the company commander and first sergeant had been fired.

At four thirty, we were all standing tall in formation when the company was called to attention by the first sergeant. If he had been fired, he looked like he liked it. Then we were told to be "at ease," a command to stand kind of relaxed but not slouching, and he said he was proud of all our hard work in getting prepared for the inspection we had just undergone. Shortly, the company commander, or CO who would normally announce the results, would come out, but then he said they were breaking that tradition; maybe the CO had gotten canned or fired this time. He then called the company to attention, and out marched the battalion commander and the company commander. If he had been fired, he looked like a rabbit that had just been set free, smiling from ear to ear. The battalion commander gave us the "at ease" command.

He then said how proud he was to be a commander of a unit like ours. "You have set the standards of excellence for our battalion and for Fort Bragg. The inspection team composed of subject matter experts from technical units and senior personnel from post headquarters are all in agreement. You have far surpassed any unit in our area they have inspected. Your training, supply, and company records were, without exception, the most accurate and complete records that they have ever checked. We all know the effort it takes to carry out daily operations and meet the regulatory requirements that are necessary for the Army to document its day-to-day operations, and because of your efforts in every area, I wanted to come and announce to you the results of your inspection. One word says it all—*outstanding*. I am proud of you, and you make me proud to be your commander. Thank you. Now your CO has, I hope, a very few words." Everyone laughed.

He said, "The only thing I have to say is I am proud to be a part of this outstanding team. I have asked our battalion commander to join us for a special steak and eggs with all the extras for breakfast. Let's hear it for out battalion commander." The raucousness could be heard all over the post. I was proud to be part of the unit, but what about Fort Polk, Louisiana?

Chapter 4

In a few days, I learned I was being assigned to a unit at Fort Polk, Louisiana. In hindsight, I now realize that God allows us new experiences to learn and grow, both from an emotional and a mental perspective. Upon arriving at Fort Polk, I was assigned duties at my new unit to record flight time on aircraft parts. Time was recorded for maintenance purposes, and as was explained and pointed out to me repeatedly, correct records and the posting of time on affected parts were critical for proper maintenance and safety. I did wonder if the job was so important, why they trusted it to a "newbie." Of course, the Army always has more than an adequate number of senior soldiers (noncommissioned officers or NCOs) looking over your backside.

Breaking into a new organization is not simple. You are the "newbie," and everyone is always checking you out. One slipup or mistake, and you get labeled, and it could take weeks, or you could never get back in with your soldier buddies. The officers and NCOs were not above getting into the game. Loyalty and never "ratting out" a fellow soldier were two rules you did not break without serious costs. Within a couple of weeks, I was being invited to go to the beer garden for a beer and hamburger with some of the guys in the unit: the first step. Even though I hated the taste of beer, at this point, I kept my mouth shut and ate my hamburger and drank my beer very slowly. Regardless, a number of the guys kept saying, "Drink up." Al, an older draftee from North Dakota, came to my defense, and as the leader of the pack, that ended the kidding and the end of the "drink up" calls. No one challenged Al. I noticed the officers and NCOs also treated him a little differently from the rest of us. The NCOs would say, "You lowlife enlisted swine," to us, but if they said it in Al's presence, I had not noticed. You see, when you are called a lowlife and they all have all the power, you just take it and go on.

Over time, Al and I became good friends and best buddies, and it was doubly good for me, no kidding, and Al was one of the few lower enlisted soldiers, privates (PVTs) through SP4s (Specialist 4 is the lowest grade for a specialist, better known as a corporal) who had a car. In fact, he was the only one in our platoon who had a car. There were three or four other lower enlisted men that had cars in other PLTs. Without "wheels," the only other transportation were the post buses and taxis, which cost too much money for PVTs. So, we all pooled our money for gas, and Al's car was our away-from-Fort-Polk chariot. One long weekend, a weekend plus a federal holiday, we all decided to go to Port Arthur, Texas, since Jim, one of the group, was from Texas and had spun some wild tales about Texas and its port cities. So Saturday after noon formation and a safety lecture by one of the officers and the first sergeant telling us not to do anything stupid, which he said he knew we would, he dismissed us for a long weekend. After all of this, we loaded up in Al's car, Al and I in front, Jim and two more of our buddies in the back, and off to Port Arthur, Texas, we went.

We arrived early evening, and as always with a group of young GIs, we were starving. As we were driving around looking for a good place to eat, a sign half as big as the building read, "The best 16 oz. T-bone steak for only $2.50 plus tax with free iced tea." Thank goodness, no free beer. The sign also read, "They may be bigger than 16 oz., but we will give you a free one if they weigh less." We all agreed that was the best deal in town. So, we pulled into the parking lot, which was about half-full, a good sign, got out of the car, and headed for the door.

The waiter said, "Howdy?" and showed us a table. He looked at our short hair and asked, "Are you guys sailors?"

As one, we all said, "No, we are soldiers from Fort Polk, Louisiana.

He hollered at a girl behind the cash register and said, "We got soldiers from Fort Polk here!"

She hollered back in the kitchen and said, "Paul, get five of our best steaks for our soldiers." She then looked at us and said, "You were going to order steaks, right?"

Again, in one voice, we all said, "Right!" We settled back as Henry, our waiter, kept our glasses full of the best tea I had since leaving home. When the steaks came out, Henry was carrying two, Paul from the kitchen had two, and the lady operating the cash register had one. We all stared in disbelief at the steaks that covered very large platters, with French fries piled high on them as well. Henry said, "You guys think you can handle these steaks?"

Again, one voice: "Right on!"

He said, "I bet you can," and with that, he left, and a few minutes later, he was back with our salads. It was a meal fit for a king. The steaks were as good as they looked, and we were a group of happy soldiers. But our meal was not over. Out came the pecan pie with ice cream on top. We all said, "We can't eat another bite."

Henry said, "See that lady over there? She ordered the pie, so please don't disappoint her." So we dug into the best pie I have ever eaten. In fact, the clown in the group, Jamie, took his dish up and licked the last drop of ice cream and pie. We had not paid attention to the other patrons, but when Jamie did his thing, the whole restaurant let out a Texas roar of approval. We all stood up, bowed, and headed toward the cash register to pay for one of the best meals we had ever eaten. Al got to the register first, but the lady said, "Your meal has been paid for. Enjoy our fine city." Al started to object, but she said, "Don't insult these fine folks. They wanted and did pay for your steaks, and you know Ms. Annabelle over there paid for your pie."

Al went over to her table, took her hand, and kissed it. Ms. Annabelle looked to be about one hundred, but you know how older people look when you are young. She stood up and gave Al a kiss on his forehead, and the crowd went crazy again. Al rejoined us, and we all bowed and saluted the crowd. They gave us an approval nod, and we left the restaurant, feeling good about ourselves as soldiers. Then it was back in Al's car to explore Port Arthur.

It did not take long before we realized Port Arthur was "dead." There were hardly anyone on the streets, few cars, fewer people, and most of the stores were closed. Something was going on. Was the fair in town, and what had emptied the place? Nothing. Jamie, the plate licker and the "nut" from New York City, said, "We need to ask a taxi cab driver where the action is. They always know." No one had a better idea. We drove around until we spotted a taxi with the driver just waiting outside a Sears & Roebuck store, one of the few places open. Al pulled in beside him and took charge as he always did when it took a cool head to get results. Al said hello to the cabbie and introduced us as a group of soldiers from Fort Polk looking for some fun. The cabbie seemed to understand what we were looking for, but for me, I was not sure what fun we were looking for, but I was not about to let the guys know.

Al was still talking to the cab driver. We all heard the cabbie say, "Boys, the Texas Rangers rode into town last week and closed down all the fun places and some places that were not fun, anyway. The streets before they came to town were so busy that it looked like New Orleans during Mardi Gras. Look at it now, dead."

Then Al pulled out his wallet and gave the driver a bill. He turned to us and said, "You four guys give me four dollars each." The cab driver then said, as if speaking just to Al, "The only place that I know that may still be in operation is the Plantation. That's where the mayor and all the bigwigs hang out for their fun. You guys follow me, and I will introduce you to the lady of the house, which just happens to be my sister. She sure makes Sunday dinner at Mama's interesting. Okay, boys, follow me."

We drove out of town and cut off on the only paved county road except the highway we had been driving on. Some things have a way of paying back that you don't suspect: a nice blacktop road. We drove down this road for what seemed like miles. Just then, a huge white plantation-looking house, all lit up, was in our view. The house looked like something from the South before the war among the states. There were no cars out front, even though the house was well lit. The cab pulled under the covered driveway and stopped at the front door. The cab driver got out, again coming back to talk to Al. Al told us to wait in the car, and they would see if they could set up anything. He was gone for a long time, or so it seemed. We began to think he had left us high and dry, but we were in Al's car, so we were not abandoned, just left out of the mix. Just then, they came out and said it was all set up. He then turned to Al and said, "You guys think you can find your way back to town? I got to make a living."

Al said, "Thanks, and yes, we can find our way back to town."

The cabbie looked at Al and said, "Ask for Savannah," and then drove off. We all headed for the front door with a new adventure high on our minds, at least for me, and I suspected for the others, except maybe Al. He stood at the door and said, "Don't you guys act like a bunch of dopes. We will go inside, pay our money, have what some call a good time, and then get the hell out of Texas with our heads held high. You get it?"

We all said yes, but again, except for Al, I was not sure anyone knew what to expect. We all then went inside and walked into a room that I had only seen in the movies. Four huge chandeliers hung from a ceiling that looked twenty feet high, and it had a stairway with wood so shiny it seemed unreal. The stairs went to a landing around the room we were in, which was large enough that two games of basketball could be played at the same time, or so it seemed, and from this landing, you could see doors leading to somewhere. We were all so awestruck by the splendor of the place we had not even seen the ladies sitting and standing around a bar at one end of the huge room, the center of the fun. The bar covered one whole end of the ground floor. The bottles and the glasses looked like a million diamonds and covered the whole end wall. It was a sight to behold by this Georgia boy just out of the cotton fields, but I kept my mouth shut. However, I noticed the other guys were as much in awe as I was, all except Al.

He started walking toward the bar, and one of the most beautiful girls I have ever seen came up to him and said, "I'm Savannah." She waved her hand at the girls around the bar and said, "We understand you guys are looking for some companionship. It has been kind of slow since the Rangers rode into town last week, so we are also in the mood for good companionship. We understand you guys are soldiers from Fort Polk. I just love to see those pictures that they take when you first join the Army, with no hair and with that serious look. Please show me your picture identification cards." Al got his wallet and pulled out his ID card. He looked at us, and we all followed suit. Savannah looked at them and then at us, smiled, and handed our ID cards back to each of us. Al later told us she was just checking to make sure we were soldiers and not Texas Rangers out to run a sting on the operation by pretending to be soldiers and then arresting everyone. We all had a good laugh when he told us that.

Now back to the Plantation. Savannah, after checking our ID cards, suggested we buy the girls a drink. We did as she suggested. The girls seemed to select who they wanted to buy their drinks. In hindsight, they were in charge. I thought I was lucky when Sally came up to me and said, "Why don't you buy me a drink so we can get to know a little about each other?" We talked over one drink, and I was in love. Her smile blocked out everything else in the room. Her voice was like music, and I would have walked over hot coals right then if she had asked. We were on our second gin when she said, "Why don't we take our drinks upstairs to my room? We don't want you to spend all your money on drinks now, do we?" The drinks were $5 each, and at that rate and a few more double drinks, I would be out of money.

I was glad to follow her suggestion. She took my hand, and up the stairs to her room we went. I was not completely dumb, but this was my first time, and I'm sure Sally was well aware of my level of experience. She closed the door and looked at me for what seemed like hours. Then she said, "This is your first time, right?" I did not lie. She smiled and said, "I'm a good teacher. The ladies in your life will thank me if they only knew." She was true to her word. She explained that all young guys, and even most of the older men, knew little or nothing about how to maximize their performance or how important mutual enjoyment of sex was to their own enjoyment. She then began the teaching process. When we had finished, she said, "You're a good student. Just remember, it takes two to tango, and you both should have a good time. Have good sex, and remember, build on what we started tonight. Please don't become a 'Wham, bam, thank you, ma'am' kind of guy. You are too good to end up like that. It hurts and cheapens everyone."

I didn't know how to proceed at this point, so I reached for my wallet, but she put her hand over my back pocket and said, "Don't, I got as much out of this as you did." We both looked at each other and started laughing our heads off. What was so funny, I don't know. Then I remembered my buddies from BCT and how they talked about good and bad sex, and I told Sally. She had another good laugh and said, "They were so right." I now kind of understood. We were in each other's arms, still laughing, as she opened the door to go downstairs. We must have taken longer than the other guys because they were all at the bar drinking five-dollar drinks. As we approached the bar, she spoke to the bartender. He gave me a drink, and she said, "Put it on my tab." The guys looked at me kind of funny. Then she kissed me and said, "I'm kind of beat. I'm going to bed." As she was going up the stairs, she said, "Come back, Rob, and I will give you a free one." With that, we both broke out into laughter. She was at the top of the stairs and waved as she walked into her room.

At that moment, I became the "stud," and when the boys got back to Fort Polk, the story only got bigger and bigger. Al and I became the two go-to guys. We all hung out at this bar in Leesville, Louisiana, called The Barn because that is about what it looked like. Anyway, we liked it. One day, Al and I were sitting at the bar, and this good-looking dark blonde girl came in and looked around. She spotted us sitting at the bar, walked over, and said, "May I join you two good-looking guys?" Of course, we said, "Please do." She sat down at the bar, and before we could ask her what she wanted to drink, she ordered a screwdriver (vodka and orange juice). She then opened her handbag, placed a fifty-dollar bill on the bar, and told the bartender to give us another of whatever we were drinking. At that time, I had never seen a fifty-dollar bill before—how time changes. She then turned to us and said, "I want to start off even."

We talked and joked. Then she told us she was new in town and was out looking for someone to talk to, and that was all. We got the message. We learned she was from Texas, and even though we talked, that was about all we learned about her. She knew that we were soldiers and, therefore, had a limited amount of money, so she insisted on buying the drinks. That was also a first for me and made my Southern pride hurt but not enough to not accept the drinks and the company of a beautiful girl. Al said he did not feel right with her buying all the drinks, so he said, "Rob, buy us all a drink." We all had a good laugh, and I bought a round of drinks. Crystal looked at me with those blue eyes and said, "I like you." There was no beating around the bush with her. She just said what she wanted to say and let the chips fall wherever they landed.

Al, Crystal, and I became good friends. She had a pink Cadillac convertible, and some of the guys saw us riding around with her, and that sealed the deal. I was the "stud," and I must admit, I enjoyed my new status, so to speak. One day, just she and I were riding around, and I got up the nerve to ask her how she made a living. She lived in a nice house in Leesville, had a new car, and had plenty of money. She looked at me and said, "I have a sugar daddy who loves me and lets me do what makes me happy. I like being with good-looking men, like you and Al, going to bars, eating at good restaurants, buying nice clothes, and in general, just hanging out with fun people like all of you." That was the end of that conversation.

Crystal and I became more of a twosome, as far as I knew. Al was dating a girl from The Barn he had met there. She was fun also. The four of us or sometimes the three of us—Crystal, Al, and myself—could be seen in town and cities all around Fort Polk. It was nothing for us to go to see an Alice Cooper concert in Shreveport, Louisiana, and end up in Dallas at a good restaurant. We all had a good time. One day, I was on kitchen police or KP duty, where soldiers helped the cooks prepare and serve meals and clean up afterwards, and Crystal drove up in her pink car at lunchtime. She was dressed and looking better than anyone you would see in the movies. She was beautiful. The guys waiting in the chow line to eat all went crazy. She got out and, before I could get to her, came over and gave me a big hug and a kiss. She then wanted to know if she could eat lunch with me and the rest of the soldiers. Al came up at that time and heard her ask about lunch. He said, "I'll find out."

Al went to the back of the mess hall or dining facility, where the NCOs and officers ate. He told the first sergeant what was going on and that Crystal wanted to eat lunch with the company. Before the first sergeant could respond, the CO said he would be happy for her to have lunch with his soldiers and that PVT Robinson could take time off from his KP duties to eat lunch with her also. We were still outside when the CO called, "At ease," and said, "We have a special guest for lunch with us today. You will all act and behave as soldiers and treat our special guest with respect." He then told Al to inform me that Crystal would be a welcome and an honored guest at lunch. She insisted, after being informed that soldiers lined up and went through a serving line to get their own food, she would do the same. She got in line and received her metal tray, which is what we ate on, and went through the serving line like the queen she was. The commander sent one of the lieutenants to inform me that I could join our guest for lunch. I thanked him and said, "Yes, sir," and all the soldiers insisted that I go ahead of them and catch up with Crystal so I could eat with her. She laughed and talked to everyone. I was surprised at how much she knew about Army life and how to joke about GI stuff. Everyone was impressed, which included the officers and the NCOs.

It was the longest lunch we ever had and, I must add, the most enjoyable one. Everyone was a captive of her charm and grace. After lunch was over and as I was walking her back to her car, she turned to me and said, "Thanks for one of the best days of my life. I will always remember this day." Then she kissed me, and I noticed a tear in her eye. I asked her, "What's wrong?" She looked at me for a while and said, "Remember you asked me how I could afford all the things I have without working and I said I have a sugar daddy who lets me do what I like to do and he pays the bills?" I said, "I remember." Another tear rolled down her cheek, and she said, "Sugar daddy is really my father, and he has cancer. He is expected to live only a few more months. I must go home and stay with him. I will miss you and Al, but our good times must come to an end. Now give me a good-bye kiss and don't make an emotional scene, you big lug. Good-bye." With that, she left me standing there as she waved good-bye to me, Al, and a hundred or so lucky soldiers standing there, who were wishing they were me. If they had only known. I told Al what was going on. He suggested that we keep it between the two of us, which was okay with me.

Nothing but work happened for the next couple of weeks. Then we got a call from someone from one of the bigger banks in Leesville who wanted to know if we could stop by the bank and see Mr. Sharpton. We said yes. Neither Al nor I knew what was up. We went into the bank, and the receptionist asked if she could help us. We informed her that we were there to see Mr. Sharpton at his request. An attitude change instantly happened. Did we want coffee? No. Would we please follow her? Yes. We followed her down a hall to a door at the rear of the building. She knocked, and a loud voice said, "Come in." She opened the door and said, "These are the two gentlemen you asked to see." Mr. Sharpton was a man that oozed authority. He looked us up and down and then asked us to be seated. "I guess you two are wondering why I wanted to see you."

"Yes," we both said. "I have a special request from an old friend of mine from Texas. I believe you know his daughter, Crystal."

"Yes," we said again."

"The house that Crystal lived in while she was here is vacant. My friend has asked me to determine if you two would benefit from living in that house while you are stationed at Fort Polk. I will pay the cost for you to live there. The only request he has is that you don't trash the place. After I looked into your backgrounds and how you treated Crystal, I'm confident you would be good stewards for that house. You see, my friend once lived there long ago, and the house will never be sold because, as he will tell you, it is part of his soul. If you men agree, the house is yours to live in as long as you are assigned to Fort Polk. What is your answer?" I looked at Al. We both said yes at the same time. Mr. Sharpton said, "Fine. Here are the keys. If you need anything, just call me. Here is my private line. I don't expect any problems." With that, he stood up and again wished us well. Then he said, "One more thing, Crystal cared for you two, and her father and I appreciate you honoring her request not to see her again. If she wishes to see you, she will do so. Again, enjoy your stay here. Good-bye."

Al and I left the bank and went to see our off-post home. Al and I talked about the strangeness of all this, and we decided to just kick back and enjoy it. I must admit I missed Crystal with a passion. We got back to the company, and it seemed everyone was in an uproar about something. We finally found James, who stopped long enough to tell us what was going on. It seemed that two of the guys in the company were caught holding each other a little too close in the shower. The rumor mill ran wild. The name-calling began, also threats, and all the mean stuff we humans are capable of started coming out. The company commander had a 100 percent formation of all assigned personnel, which meant no excuse for not being there, and he laid down the law. The two soldiers would be left alone, an investigation into their conduct had been initiated, and upon completion, a course of action would be decided by the chain of command. "Anyone in violation of this directive will be subject to disciplinary action. Is that understood?" A "Yes, sir!" from us all resounded. Then he commanded, "Dismissed," and back to work we all went.

The next day, Al and I went through the chow line, and the only two chairs available were with Mike and Shane, the two guys from the shower incident. Al looked at me, and I said, "Why not?" We went over to their table and asked if we could join them for lunch. They looked at us as if they were about to cry. Mike said, "Are you sure?" Before I could say anything, Al said, "Why not?" The mess hall went quiet. I said to Shane, "I guess you two are getting a lot of cold shoulders." He said, "You better believe it, and from some of the guys we thought were our best friends." Al said, "You never know. If Rob ever lets me down when I have trouble, I'm just going to kill him." We all had a good laugh, and I said, "He probably would too!" Then we talked about everything else except their major problem. We finished our meal at the same time, and as we all stood up to leave, Al said, "If you two need someone to talk to, Rob and I are available." Then they both looked at me, and I said in a voice loud enough to be heard, "Sure, if you need someone to talk to, count on us." That night in the barracks when we walked in, the talking stopped. Al looked at me and said, "Rob, are you sure enough about your sexuality to talk to anyone?"

"Sure, Al, and I know you are."

"What do you think? Are some people so worried about where they stand they're afraid someone might call them names like some are calling Mike and Shane? They were our soldier buddies two weeks ago."

"I guess we just forget they were okay then. Maybe it's a lack of loyalty on our part, or maybe it is because we are just afraid of what others will say about us. It has got to be something."

Al said, "What do you guys think? The 'unelected leader' and the 'stud' ate and talked with the two of them, and now they were putting the rest of us, their buddies, on the hot seat for our behavior toward Mike and Shane."

One of the guys spoke up and said, "I guess we have been a little too hard on them." Several more nodded their heads in agreement. The next day at breakfast, Mike and Shane had other soldiers talking to them, and others joined them to eat. They were not in the fold, but they could now stand the heat to come. Later, the first sergeant said, "PVT Robinson, the CO wants to see you now, so get over to his office and report."

"Yes, First Sergeant." I went to the Orderly Room, the name for offices of the first sergeant and CO, and informed the company clerk, who was sitting behind the first sergeant's desk (the first sergeant had better not catch him there) that the CO wanted to see me. He said, "Wait there while I check." He knocked, and I heard the CO say, "Come in." The company clerk said, "Private Robinson is here to see you, sir. Did you want to see him now?"

"Yes, tell him to come in." The company clerk came out and said, "Report to the CO as ordered." I knocked on the door, and the CO said, "Come in." I walked in, stood at attention, saluted, and said, "Private Robinson reporting as ordered." The CO said, "Stand at ease. I want to thank you for the courage and leadership you and Al showed by eating and talking with the two soldiers going through some hard times. I know you noticed the differences in their treatment this morning. That's what you and Al accomplished. You have put yourselves on the line for two soldiers and two human beings. That takes courage. I could not have accomplished that with all the command authority I have. I have checked with your supervisor at the airfield. He said you are doing outstanding work. I have instructed the first sergeant to ensure your promotion to PFC (Private First Class) ASAP. He will tell you when to sew on your new stripes. Keep up the good work. Again, thank you. That's all."

"Yes, sir! Thank you, sir." As I was walking out the door, the voice said, *I give you the opportunity through experiences to build a foundation from which you could help others. You have not failed me. Remember, no one has the wisdom or the knowledge to judge that which I have created. All of you are my children.* I was floating on air. I had not known that the last six months had been leading up to my actions in the last two days. Boy, was I glad to be PFC and not Private Robinson anymore.

Chapter 5

The "good times" at Fort Polk were coming to an end. Al would be getting discharged and leaving in early May, and I would follow in mid-July. Bart, an SP4 or corporal, now was going to reenlist, and we all, except Al, had been giving him a hard time and calling him a lifer. A lifer is a career soldier that we all said could not do anything else. Al stopped this by telling Bart how much he valued men and women in the armed forces. That ended the kidding right there and then. Bart went around with a big head and an expanded chest after an endorsement from Al. The first of May came so quickly, and the gang hardly had time to plan a farewell party for Al.

The Barn we all went to closed early and opened the back door for all of us. What a party. Some of the junior officers and NCOs stopped by to say good-bye but did not stay. The Army frowns on lower enlisted men and women and officers and NCOs fraternizing or partying together. We all had a good time. In all, there must have been over a hundred people there, mainly soldiers and some civilians. Al was touched and pleased at the turnout. The Army had decided that Al would be discharged on the fifth of May, not the tenth as we had expected and planned on. Leave it to the Army to change and then change again. On the morning of the fifth, Al got up early and packed his car. Then he came over to my bunk to say good-bye. I was pissed that he had not woken me up, and now he was all ready to leave. He said, "No long goodbyes from my best Army buddy." I started to speak, but he held up his hand and, without saying it, told me to keep my trap (mouth) closed. I did. He then told me how much he had enjoyed our times together and that I had made Fort Polk bearable for him. He then said, "Get out of your rack (bed) and come outside and wave good-bye, Army buddy." I got out of bed as I was told and followed Al to his packed car. I said, "Good-bye," and started to say some more when his hand went up again. He said, "No bullshit. Good-bye, buddy."

As he drove off with a wave from me and one from him, a tear rolled down my cheek. A voice—his voice—said, *Change*. I knew then friendships would form, and these friendships would only last for a time. Change. Another lesson. I decided it was time to go see Mr. Sharpton and return the keys to our house. The receptionist welcomed me and escorted me back to Mr. Sharpton's office. He even stood up, offered me a seat, and asked the receptionist to give me a cup of coffee. He never seemed to order anyone to do anything, always a request. But when he requested things, his requests were followed. Leadership, management style: we could all learn from his method. The coffee came back on a tray with sugar and cream. Thank goodness, I hate black coffee. He looked at me the same way he looked at Al and me on the first day we met. "I understand your friend Al has gone back to North Dakota."

"Yes, sir."

"Did you know that his family owns half of the state?" By the look on my face, he could tell I had not known. "They may not own half of the state, but his family has money they will never spend. When you two came into my bank, I had your families checked out. I was glad to see the report that both of you came from good stock. Crystal's father was pleased and told me he understood both of your backgrounds. He had already had you checked out when he learned that Crystal was becoming your friend. You see, his kind does not leave things to chance. If he had found you unacceptable, you both would have been out of Fort Polk so fast you would have hardly had time to pack your suitcase—sorry, your duffel bag." He laughed at what he considered a joke. I did not doubt that what he was telling me was the truth. I handed him the keys, and as he was looking at them, I told him how much Al and I appreciated living in the house. He looked up and said, "Crystal's father told me to thank you, boys, for being nice and expecting his daughter's wishes. She is going through some rough times now. She does not need the added complications that would come about by falling too much in love with one of you."

He was right: the three of us had been in love. Our friendship and memories would have to do. They were better than nothing. Then the voice said, *You are beginning to understand.* I looked at Mr. Sharpton and again thanked him and stood up to leave. He came around his desk, and I expected a handshake, but he embraced me and said, "I thank you. You are a fine American. I wish for you the best of life. Enjoy it. It will be over before you know it." I had not noticed before, but he was an old man. Then we said good-bye again, and I walked out of the bank. I was discharged on July 13, the same day of the month I had been drafted into the Army. I had decided to go back home to Georgia. My mother and father did not welcome me back with open arms but just a nod of okay.

After a month or so, I decided to travel. I had saved a little money and was off to New Orleans, Louisiana. Without the crew, my Fort Polk Army buddies, it was not the same. Change, change, change…why couldn't everything stay the same? I knew the answer without asking. I decided to leave New Orleans and go to California. I took a bus to San Francisco, and my money ran out shortly after getting there. I could not find any work, but I was on the streets with hundreds of young people my own age who knew how to survive. The missions offered free food. Some gave you vouchers for cheap hotels so you could wash up and get a good night's sleep. This allowed you to look halfway presentable the next day to look for work. No job, no money, what to do? One thing left to do was to sell your blood at the blood bank. Just my luck, I have the most common type of blood there is, and therefore, the price was the lowest. But money was money, and they gave you a free drink and a snack.

Then the voice asked, *Can you live like this? No.* By this time, I had my possessions, a few sets of clothes and some other things, in a small bag. I had given away some of my clothes to others that had even less than me. I was ready to leave San Francisco. I did not have money for a bus ticket, so I thumbed or hitchhiked out of town, and I was going back to Georgia…again. My parents again gave me the okay for my feet to go under their table and sleep in one of their beds, which was formerly my room and my bed, but in a family of ten, when you leave, you are expected to stay gone, even though other brothers and sisters had come back for short stays. My parents had always supported their children through good times and bad. Isn't that what parents do?

After about a month, my mother and father were openly talking loud enough so I could hear. They said, "He needs to get a job." So, I started looking and was hired at a local clothing manufacturing company. My job was packing men's suits in boxes to be shipped all over the US. It was considered to be one of the best jobs for the new hires because of the potential for advancement. It was the initial training for salesman jobs at the company. I lasted two weeks. What a disgrace. Mother was very upset. Dad said nothing. In all fairness, hour after hour of putting men's suits in a box became more than I wanted to handle. The conversations started again. "He needs to get a job." I thought about it and said to myself, why not rejoin the Army lifer? The voice said, *You have free will to do what you want to do.* I rejoined the Army in September and was in Heidelberg, Germany, by October, in time to go to the Oktoberfest in Munich. This was not going to be so bad. I was assigned to the signal command/signal officer for the United States Army European Command, a two-star general. I soon learned that working for him and at that level of command had its privileges. I had my own room.

We seldom worked past noon on Saturday, and Sundays were almost all free time. Life was good again. I had never owned a car, even though I had wanted one for forever. One day, as I was walking to work, I passed this British Leland dealership, and in the window was this fire-red Austen Healey 3000. I fell in love. After work that day, I stopped in and asked for the price, which was clearly on the windshield. The salesman looked at me kind of funny and said, "The price is on the windshield." I then asked how much they would sell it for. He said, "We do not negotiate. You pay what is on the windshield." I said, "In America, we don't pay what's on the windshield." He said, "You are not in America." He then laughed and asked me if I liked the car. Of course, I said I did. He then explained that they received just so many cars, and the price was set.

The next day, I went to the bank to check to see if I could borrow the money for the car. "Of course," said the loan officer. "Bring me one of your pay slips, and if nothing is being taken out of your pay, we would be glad to loan you the money to buy your car." In two days, I was driving my dream car. I had waited so long for a car, and now I had my dream car. Then the voice said, *It is sometimes better to wait than make a hasty decision and live with the consequences. Do you not think this applies to more than just your shiny new red car?* It did. Lesson learned.

The enlisted men and women assigned to the headquarters were for the most part older. There were a few of us younger guys who were on either side of twenty. Most of us had cars. In this group, there were several sports cars, and on the weekends, we would all get together and go places. One weekend, it was decided we would go to Baden, Germany, to a gambling casino. It was said to be one of the finest casinos in Germany at that time. So, off we went. The place was packed. The gambling took place on the first floor, and the dance floor was on the second floor. All the young people headed for the second floor. The older ones headed for the gambling tables. I noticed that for a lot of the couples, the men would be a lot older than the girls. This was also true for the women: old-young couples. They separated almost as soon as they came in the door—older to the tables, younger upstairs to dance.

Of course, a Georgia boy had never been in a place like that, and I thought it was nice that fathers and mothers would bring their daughters and sons with them when they went gambling. When I told my new buddy from New York what I thought, he almost died laughing. He then said, "I got to look out for you. Don't get me wrong, but you're the dumbest guy I know when it comes to some things. Why do you think we can be dancing, and then when one of the staff comes up and says something to the girl, she will stop dancing and leave?" Then it hit me: they were not sons and daughters but…whatever. My buddy just shook his head and headed for this good-looking blonde girl who had just come up the stairs. The voice said, *Things are not always as they appear. What you see is sometimes determined by what you know and what you have experienced. Go and have a good time. There's a good-looking girl over there trying to get your attention.*

The next few months went off without much excitement. Then one of the guys wanted to go to Auschwitz and see the crematoriums. So, off we went. The horror of the place was still real. None of us could believe what we were seeing and hearing from the guide as to what went on. You could see much of the camp had been destroyed or torn down. But there was enough to see and kind of understand what happened to thousands of people. How could a people be led to take part in something like this? The camp, the roads, and the rail lines were in plain sight. They were not hidden. They were in plain view. How had a people become so despised that several countries and their citizens saw but did not see, heard but did not hear, thought but did not think, felt but did not feel, turn off all their/our human traits, values, and, yes, become as the lowest form of animals those that kill their own kind?

The voice replied, *You have answered your own question. In the history you have seen and experienced today, you have seen a part of me that many call total evil, but I must remind you that thousands knew, endorsed, and supported these actions. That is your free will, and it does reflect a part of me. The history of mankind is replete with examples of this type of behavior. Your free will by my design gives you the freedom to act and do as you please, but be aware that others may use their free will to control and destroy. Societies are formed, and laws are passed to control freewill actions that affect communities. Again, history has many examples of communities working together to live in harmony with their values after events you have witnessed. Do not judge too quickly that which you are capable of and can become a willing participant.* End of thought.

Boy, what a day. There was little talk on the way back to Heidelberg, Germany, our home. The next day was a Monday, and it was back to work. Nothing much happened for a few months, just going to work, getting off work, going out to eat, drinking, and partying with friends. Then one day, the deputy signal officer, who was a full colonel, called me into his office and said, "I have been looking over your personnel file and think you would make a good candidate for Officer Candidate School." He asked me if I had thought about going to OCS and becoming an officer. I said I would think about it. His secretary knocked on the door and said to him, "You have a meeting in ten minutes at post headquarters." He said, "Thanks," and got up to go but not before saying, "Think about OCS, and we will talk some more."

"Yes, sir!" I said. He was out of the door. His secretary said to me, "If you don't keep him on schedule, he would never be on time for anything." Boy, how nice it must be to have someone keep you on track.

About two weeks later, he saw me walking down the hall and said, "Come into my office, Specialist Robinson."

"Yes, sir," I said.

"Have you thought about going to OCS?"

"Yes, sir."

"Well, what is your answer?"

"I think I would like to go, sir."

"Good." He hollered out to the adjoining office to no one in particular to have the adjutant come to his office. In about one minute, the captain adjutant appeared with a notebook and a pencil at the ready. The colonel said, "Specialist Robinson has decided to go to

OCS. Help him fill out the application with a forwarding endorsement from me and the general. Do you have any questions?"

"No, sir."

"You two get with it. I want the application out of here by the end of the week." The captain turned to me as we were walking down the hall and asked me, "How do you know the colonel?" "Sir, I don't."

"He must see something in you. You are the first one he has ever directed me to help fill out an application to OCS." The application was signed by me and endorsed by the signal and deputy signal officer of Europe. I did not know at the time, but with that kind of horsepower behind an application, you may as well pack your bags. Within a month, I was approved for Infantry OCS with a reporting date of June 1. I said good-bye to all my friends and shipped my dream car back to the US, and I was on my way to Fort Benning, Georgia, home of the infantry. I picked up my car, which had been shipped to the port in New York, and headed south. I stopped by my home in North Georgia and told my parents not to worry because I was only going to stay a few days and then was heading south to Fort Benning, Georgia, for Infantry OCS. They both looked relieved and had a little laugh at my attempt to be funny.

I reported to OCS on a Sunday. I thought Sunday would be slow and give me a chance to unpack and get ready for Monday, the day OCS was going to start. I was in for a big surprise. No day of rest, even on Sunday! OCS was like BCT and airborne training rolled into one but with an added twist. You were never left alone to get your head clear and your body time to rest. The cadre came into our rooms at all times during the day and night to inspect and check to ensure we had not brought in pogey bait or food that we were not authorized to have. As young men who ran, did push-ups, sit-ups, and other forms of exercise all day, we stayed in need of food. Just don't get caught with it. Some of my Catholic buddies in OCS said the Catholic nuns did not hold up a figure to the OCS cadre if they spotted you sleeping or not paying attention in class. The general punishment was a ruler across your head and then standing on one foot in the back of the class, and you had better not fall over. Your leg, the one you were standing on, hurt so bad you were almost ready for punishment, any punishment. Just let both legs be on the ground. OCS had been going on for fourteen weeks with this type of training, which never seemed to end.

I had not adjusted to the training methods, even though I was doing well in the school. In the fourteenth week, I had received an award from my former commander, the general. The battalion commander had me come to his office, and when I reported to him, he threw the award across the table and informed me that this did not make me special. He then instructed me to take my award and not to waste any more of his time. His actions hurt, for you see, I respected my former commander, and to me, this was a lack of respect. The more I thought about it, OCS became less and less important to me. A voice from my past, my old buddy from BCT, said, "Don't be afraid to walk away if you think that is best for you."

The next week, I requested withdrawal from OCS. The battalion commander sent for me, and when I reported to him, he wanted to know if I was sure withdrawal from OCS was what I wanted to do. He informed me that my records and reports from the OCS cadre put me in the top 10 percent of all the candidates. He said he would tear up my application, and I could go back to OCS. By this time, I knew how the Army works, and I said, "I would withdraw my request if he would not set me back because of what they call motivation." He informed me he did not make deals. It was my decision. I told him I had made a decision and would stick with it. He smiled and said, "I thought that would be your answer by looking at your records. You would have made an outstanding officer. I wish you much success in your life. Please close the door on your way out." I left his office, reported to the personnel officer, and was placed on order to go back to Germany, but this time, I was going to Berlin. I was happy again—no running, sit-ups, push-ups, or whatever. I was human again. I left for Berlin, Germany, within two weeks, just enough time to say good-bye to my parents and put my dream car up on blocks for the next eighteen months, which was the time I had left on my enlistment. I flew into Berlin and was picked up at the airport by someone from my new assignment. This assignment turned out to be Headquarters Berlin Command. The soldier who picked me up dropped me off at the personnel office at my new command. There they informed me where I would be working and took me to my new section. Everyone seemed glad that I was there. Bill, a member of my new section, stood up and told the major in charge he would be glad to take me around and get me settled.

"Thanks, Bill. That sounds like a good idea." Bill looked at me and said, "Let's go."

Bill had a car, and he drove me over to the company where I would be sleeping. We went to the orderly room, and the first sergeant looked me up and down and then turned to Bill and said, "Meet your new roomie."

Bill said, "That's fine by me."

The first sergeant said, "Give Specialist Robinson his pass card and have him sign for his bedding."

I said, "Thanks," to the company clerk and signed the forms. The first sergeant told Bill to keep me straight and, if I needed anything, to let him know.

Bill said, "Yes, First Sergeant." We went up to our room, and Bill helped me unpack. My bed had been made up—a nice trick—and we were unpacked and were ready to get out in about ten minutes to see Berlin. Even though Berlin is a large city, at that time, you could see all the places that were interesting to GIs in about two hours. We drove to where you could see the Berlin Wall and then took a swing down through the middle of the city. Bill never stopped talking. He pointed out the Berlin U. Baud rail system and explained how the city bus system and the taxi system worked. Overall, he said, the transportation system was better than any of our big cities. You could tell Bill loved Berlin.

In a few weeks, I had gotten to know most of the guys, the soldiers, in the headquarters. They were all serious about doing their jobs, but most, if not all, were big-time partiers; I was becoming one of them. We constantly had security briefings on the Russian spy net and things we should report and places we should not go. Of course, our favorite bar was one of the places not to go, but it was never placed under off-limits. I guess both sides had their spies working the place. The funniest thing to happen about spies was when a soldier we knew defected to the Soviet Union. He had fallen in love with a girl from the bar, and she had taken him into East Germany, and from there, he decided to defect to the Soviet Union. In about a week, as the rumor went, the Soviets called our side and said, "If you want your defector back, pick him up on so-and-so street at blank hours." Of course, as the rumor went, they said one of the Soviet's black sedans slowed and almost stopped, and out came our defector. We all agreed the reason they did not keep him was because they did not want to feed him for what they could find out from him. I'm not sure that was correct. He was a clerk in a sensitive job.

Regardless, our side had him back. Berlin was a fun city, the job was good, and most importantly, I had a group of friends. Life was good for me again. There was a small hotel near the bar where all of us hung out, and they served the best sauerbraten or meat with gravy that any of us had ever eaten. So, it became an almost daily stopover on our way to or from the bar. They had a young German, about our age, waiting on tables, and some of the guys gave him a hard time. The war was over, and all of us, including the Germans, were now trying to get on with our lives. I tried to get Hans, the German waiter, to come out and drink with us. However, he always refused, saying that the hotel manager would fire him for socializing with guests, even those who ate at the restaurant. I respected the rules Hans had to follow, and I surely did not want to make trouble for him.

We continued to eat there, and I tried to keep the guys as civil as possible. I could understand how the "ugly American" idea came to be. We could be demanding, condescending, and just downright rude. At that time, America was riding high as the unquestionable leader of the world. My enlistment was almost over, along with two other guys from our group, and Bill was planning a big farewell party for all of us. I stopped off at the Post Exchange or PX, a big store, on my way to the party, and they had a special on wristwatches. I decided to buy one for Hans for all the trouble we had given him and how he had remained a good sport through it all. The clerk asked me if I wanted it gift-wrapped, and I said, "No, just give me a small sack to put it in."

I stopped by the restaurant, and saw Hans was working. I sat down at one of his tables (all of us always sat in his area), and he came over to get my order. Of course, I wanted sauerbraten, which I ordered. He came back with the largest order of sauerbraten I had ever seen. I told him, "Now, that will get you fired." He said, "I know the cook." I knew he and the cook were very good friends, and both of them came from a small island in the North Sea. We both had a good laugh, and then he left to wait on another guest. I finished my meal and was waiting on my check, but no check came. Finally, I caught Hans' attention and told him to give me my check. He looked at me and said, "That's our going-away present." He then told me that he appreciated me keeping everything under control and how Albert, the cook, and he thought this was a good gift. I told him to thank Albert, and now I wanted to give him a gift to say good-bye. I handed the bag to him before he could say anything or refuse to take it. He took the bag, looked inside, and took out the watch case. His whole face lit up at the sight of the new Bulova watch. He started to say, "I can't." Before he could finish, I said, "Put it on, and don't say anything but good-bye and good luck," something I learned from Al. We both looked at each other, two friends saying good-bye. Change, change, change—that was life.

I went to the bar, and Bill had done it up right. The party was a big success, if you call everyone drinking too much and acting completely crazy a successful party. It was a great party. The three of us left Berlin two days later. I was on my way back to Georgia with no clear plans. The bad penny returns home. My parents did not seem to mind. In fact, they seemed glad to have me home. I got my dream car running and was kind of looking for work. The car was no longer important, so I sold it. That gave me money to live on while I decided what to do. In Berlin, I had met some people who worked for the US State Department, so I decided to apply for work with the US Foreign Service. I was hired in about a month. While training in Washington, I was privileged to see President Kennedy. He used the State Department's Press Room for a news conference, and all of us were allowed to go down to the basement and wave at him when he arrived. He was the first man I had ever seen in makeup. Of course, by then, I knew that most people that appeared on TV wore heavy makeup. President Kennedy took the time to come over and shake hands with most of us. I noticed he seemed to pay more attention to the good-looking girls—the better-looking, the more attention. So what? He was young and good-looking himself, even with makeup.

There was one girl in a wheelchair. He went up to her, said something in her ear, and then kissed her forehead. The crowd went wild with cheers, and he became "our" President. The other thing that stood out was the time that Vice President Johnson was going overseas on some official trip, and some of us were paid fifty dollars each to work on a Saturday and pack his things. We were given a list of things to be packed and directions about how they were to be packed. I was to pack his pillows, seal them in a plastic bag, and hand them to the person inspecting and packing everything to be taken and loaded onto his plane. It was the easiest fifty dollars I have ever made. You see, Vice President Johnson did not sleep on pillows that someone else had slept on. He had to have his own pillows. Ever since then, I inspect the pillows at hotels and motels to see if they look clean. Some of them don't, and I can now understand why he wanted his own pillows.

After a few more weeks of training, I was assigned to the American consulate in Frankfort, Germany. Going back to Germany was almost like going home. I was picked up at the airport and driven to the Consulate, where I was introduced around and met my new boss. Then I was taken to my quarters, my new apartment. I did not know what to expect. When Dirk, the guy taking me around, said, "As a single guy, you only receive a one-bedroom apartment," I was in for a big surprise. The apartment was completely furnished. It had a full kitchen, a large living room, a bathroom, and a bedroom that had two full-size beds. The Army never lived like this. I was moving up in the world. Then the voice said, *Not everyone lives like this. This does not make you better, but it can lead you down the road to think so.*

Dirk said, "It takes a little time to get used to the fact that we (meaning consulate personnel) are treated first class."

I turned to Dirk and said, "I can handle it for a while." We both had a good laugh, and he said, "So can I." The work was not hard, and the free time was great. I really liked it there. After some time, it became cold.

Thanksgiving was only a few days away. I had been there for three months, and everyone was making plans for Thanksgiving, but even though I had been invited to several of the dinners, I decided to go to Berlin. If there is anything the Army gets right every time, it is the Thanksgiving dinner. I was looking forward to seeing how many of my old friends were still there. I was kind of disappointed when I discovered Bill had left a month earlier, and most of the other guys I really liked had also departed in the months that I had been away. Frank was still there, and we were both glad to see each other and tell old "war stories" about days gone by—change, change, change. I was learning to accept and live with it. Each new day brought a new adventure. I could not relive or change the past and could only anticipate the future. Then the voice said, *You are learning.*

The protocol section of the consulate had made my hotel reservation on Berliner Strauss. I walked up to the front desk to check in, and who was there to greet me but Hans. He was now back in Berlin, working the front desk. I was glad to see him, and for a German who does not express emotions, he appeared glad to see me. He said my room was ready. He motioned for a guy to pick up my bag—I only had one—and take it to my room. I said to Hans, "I can carry my bag." He said, "Remember the rules." We both smiled, and I let the guy pick up my bag: rules. Then a well-dressed man came out of a door behind the front desk, and Hans was all business again: rules. Same rules applied: no fraternizing with guests, on or off duty.

I came back to Berlin several times during the winter and always stayed at what I called Hans' Hotel. In March, as Hans was checking me in, I said, "It's about time you and Albert took me out in Berlin." He surprised me by saying, "Okay." I said, "What about the rules?" He then told me that he and Albert would be going home for the summer to work. The well-dressed man came out, and Hans introduced me to him. He was the manager and, Hans told me later, part owner of the hotel. He greeted me warmly, and Hans told him that he and Albert were going to show me Berlin. The man smiled and said, "You would have had to take me along if I were twenty years younger." We all had a good laugh. What about the rules? No rules seemed to apply among friends.

Hans, Albert, and I had a ball for the next two nights. How they woke up and went to work the next day, I will never figure out. After the second night of partying, I had to get up and catch my flight back to Frankfort at 14:00 hours, two o'clock in the afternoon. It was all I could do to get out of bed. I finally got dressed, packed my bag, and went down to check out. Hans was at the desk, looking as if he had not been out partying at all the night before. I walked up to the desk, and the manager came out and spoke in German to Hans and then shook my hand, smiled, and said, "We are honored to have you as our guest." He then turned and went back into his office. Hans had not handed me the bill. I looked kind of funny, and Hans informed me that the man had just told him my stay was on the hotel. I started to protest, but Hans said, "Shut up and just say good-bye." I said, "Good-bye, and I will see you later." Hans said, "I hope so."

I was on my way back to Frankfort, and Hans and Albert would be going back home for the summer. Change.

Chapter 6

Time did not stand still, working all summer, and I had some vacation days saved up, so I decided to go to Berlin, my adopted city, where I had enjoyed so many good times. The flight to Berlin had been smooth and uneventful. I found my bag and walked out front to where the taxis were waiting, got into one, and handed the driver the name and address of the hotel which the protocol section at the consulate had made the reservation. The driver looked at me in his rearview mirror and, in excellent English, said, "That is a good hotel. It is close to everything, and make sure you try their Berliner Himbeergeist (which is a mixture of beer and raspberry brandy)." I thanked him, and the voice said, *Do not think you are better than anyone else.* It was a good reminder; I was kind of feeling my oats. In fact, I was beginning to think I might be just a little bit better than some people with my new job at the consulate and being treated "first class," or so I thought.

We arrived at the hotel, and the driver got out to open my door, but before he could do so, I had already grabbed my bag and was standing outside his cab to pay him. My hand went out to shake his hand and ask how much the fare was. He looked at me, and I paid him and added a 20-percent tip. He then said, "I wish all my guests were like you. Thank you (he could have said, "*Danke schon*") and have a good time in our city." With that, he got back behind the wheel and drove off, and as he was leaving, he smiled and waved. He made me feel good as I went through the doors of the hotel, which were being held open by two old men, whom I now realize were not really that old; I was just young. I walked up to the front desk and was about to say my name when the front desk manager said, "Welcome to our hotel, Herr Robinson," and turned around. What a surprise—Hans, my German friend and the waiter, was now a desk manager in a fine hotel in the center of Berlin.

We shook hands, and I noticed Hans was wearing the watch I had given him. I said, "I guess the same rules still apply, or can you take me to all the hot spots in Berlin?"

He laughed and said, "I'm afraid they do. But I will give you a map and show you where to go." I said thanks, and he said, "I took the liberty of filling out your guest reservation, so please sign here." I signed the form, and Hans motioned for someone to take my bag. I said, "Thanks, but I will carry it myself."

Hans laughed and said, "You never change."

The porter took me up to my room, unlocked the door, and handed me the key. There was a basket of fruit on the table, which I learned later that Hans had put there, and after the porter checked everything twice, I tipped him and said, "Good night." What a surprise—Hans working at the hotel, at a hotel where I had not even made the reservations. At breakfast, another surprise—Albert, Hans' friend and the cook at the other GI hotel, was a cook here. I soon learned that he also was moving up in this world. He was now a chef in charge of a shift. That morning, it just happened to be breakfast. He came out of the kitchen carrying a tray of food fit for a king and set it down on my table. I rose, gave him a bear hug, and told him how good it was to see him and Hans. We both laughed, why, I do not know. I felt it was just old buddies meeting again. He looked around at the other guests and said, "I had better get back to work. Please enjoy your breakfast." I smiled again and said, "You bet I will. Thanks. See you later." And with that, he was gone.

The other guests by that time were looking at me as if I were someone special. I could feel the voice saying, *See.* I came back several times that winter to the hotel, and each time, I got the same treatment. I even managed to get the same cab driver several times, and he would take me to special places in Berlin, but the fare was always the same, and he would not accept any more of my money than I had paid him the first time. He had shown me a picture of his two "kinder," a boy and a girl. Both looked less than ten years old. On one of my visits, I went to the Army PX in Berlin since, as a government employee, I could still shop there and bought the boy a baseball bat, ball, and glove. For the girl, I was a little lost, but the German salesclerk said, "Every little girl would love to have this doll." It was, I must admit, very beautiful. She gift-wrapped both presents, and I took them back to the hotel with me. I told Hans what they were, and I wondered if it were possible to get the cab driver that had been driving me around to drive me to the airport the next day. Hans said, "Don't worry. He will be here to drive you to the airport." Hans would have made a fine officer in their Army or ours; he just got the job done, no nonsense.

The next morning, my cab driver was waiting for me. I had not realized it, but it was the first of December, so when I handed the packages to the driver, I said, "It's a little early, but here is a small gift for your kinder for Christmas." He started to protest, but I said, "We have to get to the Tempelhof Airport. Let's go." He smiled and said okay. When we arrived at the airport, he did not want any payment, but he had not turned off the meter, so I paid him what was on the meter plus 20 percent. I then said, "I will see you before Christmas or just after New Year's. You can check with Hans at the hotel as to when I can come back." He said okay. I rushed into the airport to check in. I was running a little late, but I made it. The consulate business was slow, so I decided to ask for leave and spend New Year's in Berlin, which had become my adopted city.

Hans and Albert were glad to see me. The hotel had a big New Year's party for the guests, but the guests and staff were still separated because there was no fraternization. Even with those rules, we still had a good time. The next morning, my room phone rang. It was Hans. He said, "You have a guest to see you," and hung up before I could ask who it was. My Army buddies had all gone home by this time, so I dressed and went downstairs to meet my mystery guest.

Standing in the lobby were my cab driver with two kids, the two kids in the picture, his kinder. The smile on my face said how pleased I was to see them. I walked over to Herr Schmidt, my cabbie, and shook his hand. The little boy put his hand out and said, "I'm pleased to meet you." The little girl, who bowed with a curtsy of a queen, said, "My family would like to invite you to our house for dinner with us." No one would or could refuse an invitation like that, so I said, "I would be delighted to have dinner with your family." Hans handed me a bottle of cognac and said, "Enjoy your day."

Herr Schmidt was driving his car, not the cab. We all got into the car, and as soon as we started on our trip, the talking never stopped. The two kids spoke excellent English. I spoke some German, which gave them a good laugh. We arrived at their home, a well-kept but small house. Mrs. Schmidt had the place smelling so good that it would have made you hungry, even if you had just eaten, which I had not; I was starving. The boy had to show me his room and the baseball bat, glove, and ball I had given him. According to him, they were the best gifts ever. The girl showed me her doll and said she had named her Helen after Helen of Troy because she was so beautiful. We sat down, and all of us told stories about our lives. Herr Schmidt, his wife, and I had a good drink from the bottle of cognac that Hans had given us. The kinder, after several pleas, were given a small drink. It was a good day.

On the ride back to the hotel, Herr Schmidt, with family in tow, told me how much it meant to have an American like me come to their home. He said he wanted his kids to see that all Americans did not dislike them. He also said that some Germans were having a hard time getting over the war. Both the kids had gone to sleep during the ride, so I said, "I'm sure some of the Americans are having a hard time too. I just hope we can grow to enjoy each other as friends, and when your children get our age, it will only be history to them." We were at the hotel. I got out before Herr Schmidt and his wife did, but they both got out. Mrs. Schmidt hugged me and said, "Thank you. The gifts meant so much to the children." I shook hands with Mr. Schmidt and said, "Good-bye." They both waved as they drove off. The kids were still sound asleep. We all had a good day. Then the voice said, *See, kindness has its rewards.*

I did not get back to Berlin until the end of March. This time, Hans and Albert were getting ready to go back home to work for the summer. For this trip, I bought both Hans and Albert much better watches. I knew both of them would like them, and I was sporting one just like theirs. I checked in at the hotel. Hans was not at the desk. I was kind of disappointed. The porter took me to my room and had the key in his hand but did not move to unlock the door. Instead, he just turned the handle and threw the door open. Hans and Albert were both in the room. Both of them grabbed me and said, "Let's go party!" Afterwards, we rolled over the floor, laughing our heads off, just to see old buddies. I said, "Wait a minute," and took out two small gift-wrapped presents. I handed one to Hans and the other to Albert. After they took off the wrapping paper, they could see the cases. Inside each of the boxes was the Seiko dream watch. They both looked surprised. I said to Hans, "Give me back that piece of s——t I gave you last time."

He said, "No, I'm keeping it!"

I held up mine and said, "Mine works." They looked and slid theirs on, and then we were at it again.

Albert said, "Let's go get something to eat." The porter was still standing there watching us. I was going for my wallet when he said, "Not this time," and was gone before I could get my wallet out to pay him. Hans and Albert both laughed and said, "You don't have to pay us or bring us gifts. We just like you." Again we all burst out into laughter, and Albert said, "But thanks for the watch." Again there was laughter. The three of us had three days of partying, and Hans and Albert had to leave on the fourth day. I would rest one more day and leave on the fifth day. Just before Hans and Albert left, Hans gave me a sheet of paper with their full German names spelled out, their phone numbers, and Hans' home address with a short note written by both of them, which said how much they would like for me to visit them at their home on the North Sea. I read the note, looked at both of them, and said, "I will be there this summer." They both said together, "We will hold you to that promise." We said good-bye and that we would see each other that summer.

April and May were long months for us at the consulate, but by the end of May, the work had slowed, and I asked for leave for the first week in June. The leave was approved, and I went to the protocol section, told the German lady in charge that I was going to visit a German family, and asked what I should do. She asked a thousand questions. Then she suggested I carry the lady of the house an expensive box of candy and a smaller box of the same candy for Hans' sister. She even knew the kind of candy sold in the PX and suggested what I should get, even though Germany has some of the best chocolate candies in the world. I said okay. Then she suggested I get Hans' father a box of the best cigars. She also knew the best the PX sold. Again I said okay. Then I asked, "What about Hans and Albert?" She said, "I don't think you need to take them anything." Again, okay.

I left for Sylt on the North Sea after calling Hans to make sure it was an okay time to visit. I knew he worked for his father, and I did not want to cause trouble. Hans laughed after I told him my concerns. "You will be welcome, and my father will get a good laugh about your concerns. I or someone else will meet you at the train station." I gave Hans all the information, my arrival time, and the train I was coming on. The scheduled trains had names, again something I knew nothing about. I arrived just after dark at the station in Sylt, picked up my baggage, and was looking around for Hans or Albert, but neither was there. I was beginning to think, *What am I going to do?* Just then, an older gentleman came up to me and, in broken English, said, "Herr Robinson?" I said, "Yes, sir." He smiled and started to pick up my bag. I said, "*Danka,*" and grabbed it myself. He smiled again and motioned for me to follow him.

We went outside, and his car was waiting in front of the station. He opened the back door for me to get in, but I just tossed the bag in and opened the front passenger door. We both got in, and off we went. The moon had come up and provided enough light to kind of see the island. It was beautiful. We soon arrived at this nice brick house. I wondered why we were stopping. It did not take long to find out. The driver was out, had my bag, and was headed for the front door before I could even start to get out. He opened the front door and waited for me to get out and catch up with him. He knew the house well, for he started down a hall from the living room, opened a door, and motioned to me to come into the room. He was opening my bag and hanging up my clothes. I am sure I was just standing there dumbfounded. He patted the bed to let me know I was going to sleep there. My bedroom even had a full bathroom, which I could not believe. Some of the lower-cost hotels did not have full bathrooms. I was getting the VIP treatment, or so I thought. The driver took me outside, and I could hear music and laughter coming from a large multistory building just up the street.

In broken English, he said the Hoffmans were there, pointed at the building, and indicated that we would just walk to it. There was a path that led from the house to what I soon learned was a hotel and bar. Even though the protocol lady had said I should give the Hoffmans their gifts upon arrival, since they were not in what I suspected was their home, I placed the candy and cigars on the table with a short thank-you note for allowing their son to invite me for a few days. We walked to the building, and my driver opened the double doors and said in a loud voice, "Welcome to the Sea Gull." The Hoffmans—father, mother, and daughter, without Hans—came over to greet me. Mr. Hoffman explained that Hans was working elsewhere but would join us later. He made a place at his table and ordered beer for all of the people around the table. "These are some of my guests also," he said. His English was better than mine. We drank beer, and everyone talked at the same time. When I looked confused, Mr. Hoffman would explain what was being said. Even though the conversations were mostly in English, I still had a hard time following all the give-and-take between them.

They all seemed to be old friends. From their conversations, I gathered this was not the first time all of them had been guests of the Hoffmans.

A French girl, Lisa, kept talking to me and had taken Mr. Hoffman's place at keeping me up to speed as to what was going on. She was one beautiful girl, and everyone paid her a lot of attention. This had been going on for about an hour when Hans and Albert arrived. They both grabbed me in a bear hug, and we all had a good laugh about how friends greeted each other. Hans and Albert were each handed a beer by Mr. Hoffman, and Hans said to him, "We had a good night at the Sands." Mr. Hoffman nodded, and that was the end of their conversation. Hans, Albert, and Mr. Hoffman began to sing drinking songs, and I knew this was going to be one hell of a party. After each song, Mr. Hoffman would tell a story. Some were about his family, others were about visitors that had been guests at their home or the Sea Gull, Sands, or Sun Dance, which I gathered were hotels or something like that. Then his voice said, *Enjoy your new friends. Some of them have been through some very hard times. It does them no harm to let off a little steam. Just remember: you are not the judge of human behavior.* I did not need any encouragement. I had always been a two- or three-beer drinker, and I must have had four or five by that time. I was feeling no pain.

It was fun watching everyone have a good time. I heard Mr. Hoffman say, "Texas," and I perked up my ears. He was talking about farmwork in Texas. He then explained he had been a POW during the war and had been interned at a POW camp in Texas. I was beginning to worry. Mr. Hoffman looked at me and saw the worry on my face. He burst out laughing, came over, grabbed me, and said, "Those were some of the best years of my life! I was treated with respect and kindness, even though families in the community were losing sons in the war. I learned much from the compassion and the dignity of those Texas folks. When I got back to Germany after the war and started my hotel and restaurant business, I made a pledge to always treat other people as I had been treated in Texas." With that story, he hugged me again and said, "Everyone, have a drink on me and let's toast to friendship."

The party went on to well after midnight, and Hans and his sister escorted me to, I guessed, their home and said good night. The next morning came early, and someone was knocking on my door. It was Lisa, the French girl from the night before. She said, "Hurry, get ready. Bring your bathing suit. We will eat breakfast first with the Hoffmans, and then we will go to the beach." The Hoffmans were seated at a long table in the Sea Gull with two or three of the people from the night before. When we came in, Mr. Hoffman got up to seat Lisa and indicated I should sit next to her. Albert and two other young men came in carrying trays of food. The food was outstanding, there were all kinds of meat, hard-boiled eggs, fruit, and bread and butter that was out of this world. After we started eating, Mr. Hoffman said to Lisa, "I guess you, Rob, and the other guests will go to the beach."

Lisa said, "Yes, sir."

He then turned to Albert and said, "Pack a lunch and have it delivered to them at about thirteen hundred hours." He looked at me, grinned, and said, "How's that for military time?"

I said, "It sounds like soldier talk."

He laughed. He turned to his daughter and said, "You had better be off, or you will miss the train and a day of school." She stood up, gave him a kiss, and was gone. Mr. Hoffman pulled out one of the cigars that I had bought him and said, "Thank you." Mrs. Hoffman said, "The candy is just the kind I love, thank you."

Lisa, five or six others, and I headed for the beach. As we were walking, we passed another hotel, and I looked up and saw the sign, "The Sands." From my expression, Lisa said, "You don't know the Hoffmans very well, do you?" I told her how Hans, Albert, and I had become friends and that Hans had invited me to visit them. She laughed and said, "Let me fill you in. The Hoffmans own The Sands, The Sea Gull, and the Sun Dance. Those are the three nicest hotels on the island. You and I are staying in their home because we are 'special' guests. I wondered what made you special. Your story clears all that up. You are special! Let's go get some sun."

We made it to the beach, and the sun was great, but the water was still a little cold for me. But Lisa seemed to enjoy it. We lay in the sun, she swam, and when I got too hot from lying in the sun, I would jump in the water to cool off; it would only take about two seconds! Lisa would laugh and call me chicken (I think!). Our lunch arrived on time, and the young guy who brought the lunch could not keep his eyes off Lisa. After he left, I said, "I think you have captured another heart." She laughed and said, "No, that's just lust." We both laughed. I had never been around girls who spoke their minds like Lisa and the other European girls I had met. I liked their upfront manner.

After lunch, we decided to walk along the beach. After a while, we came upon a large sign in German and a few stones that went from the dunes to the edge of the water. Lisa just kept walking. I asked her what the sign said, and she said, "Don't worry about it," and laughed. I knew she was up to something. In the short time I had been with her, she believed in having fun, so we just kept walking. About one hundred yards from the sign and stones, an irate woman came up to us, completely naked, not a stick of clothing on or even a towel, and said something in German. She pointed to the way we had come, looked at me, and motioned to me to take off my clothes. Lisa said something to her and was laughing so hard I could have killed her. She then explained as we were walking back out of the area that it was a natural beach or, in other words, a nudist beach, and the lady was only telling us if we wanted to stay in that area, we had to disrobe. "I told her you were an American and was just getting used to our ways. She said, 'Well, have him take of his swim trunks. This old lady likes to see good-looking young men in their natural state.' I told her, 'I don't think he would be up for it.'"

I laughed and said, "Not today!" Lisa then laughed and said, "This will make a fine story for tonight's drinking party." I said, "Don't you dare!" I knew she would, though, and she did. Everyone had a good laugh and made like they were taking off their clothes, but no one did, thank goodness! By the third day, I, Lisa, and the others had explored the whole island. There were several concrete bunkers from the war that were still in good shape. The Italian couple did not talk much, but both had lost family members in the war. Lisa never discussed the war or her family's involvement or lack of involvement. The other two just said it was a bad time for all of them, and as kids, they only wanted it to end. I kept my opinions to myself and said only that I had two older brothers in the war but that neither of them was killed. Lisa then stepped in and came up with something fun to do, and "the war" was over for that day.

On the fourth day, I had to leave on the last train to get back to Frankfurt and go to work. The Hoffmans had planned an early dinner meal for my departure. Lisa, Hans, Albert, and the other guests were there. It was a feast. As we sat eating, I was seated next to Mr. Hoffman, and I could not keep from asking him about Hans working first as a waiter and then as a desk manager in hotels in Berlin. He looked at me again and said, "It is quite simple. Hans will own all that we have someday, and I want him to know the hotel business from the people who clean the toilets to the people who own and manage hotels. I think that is the only way you can fully understand what a person is going through, such as when you ask a worker to stay late and miss his child's birthday party, or when you call someone in to clean up after a drunken guest. I have done all those things, and I am proud to say Hans is following in my footsteps. When Hans and Alfred told me about you as a guest in the hotel in Berlin back when Hans waited on tables and Albert cooked and you treated them with respect and dignity, I told Hans that you were 'good people.' Then when you came back to Berlin and met Hans as a desk manager, he called and told me you were a guest in their hotel. I was pleased. He also told me about your friendship with the German cab driver and his family. On your last visit, when Hans invited you to come and visit him, I was pleased. It has been hard on some Germans and their families, but thanks to Americans like you, we are all working through these difficult times. Now, when will you be coming back to visit us?"

He kept me in his stare until I said, "Late July or early August." He said, "We will hold you to that promise." I said good-bye to the Hoffmans—Hans, Albert, and Lisa—and waved to all of the others. The driver was waiting to take me to the train station. Lisa came over, kissed me, and said, "I will see you in late July." I was off to the train station. What a four-day visit. His voice said, *Your life will be filled with ups and downs because you choose to respect others and share with them not only gifts but yourself. You have been rewarded with a time to remember.*

I was a guest at the Hoffmans in July and again in September. Each time it seemed better than the time before. When I left in September, Hans told me he would be going back to Berlin in late October. Both he and Albert had gotten jobs for the winter there. He said he would send the name of the hotel and everything later. I said okay. The Hoffmans told me that the Sea Gull stayed open during the winter, and I would be a welcome guest if I wanted to see the North Sea in the winter. I thanked them and told them I would think about it. Again I told them of my pleasure and enjoyment at meeting them and becoming friends. We all said our good-byes. Lisa had not been there. I missed her something awful. I was on the train back to Frankfurt. His voice said, *Change is coming.* I had a sick feeling in my stomach. Somehow I knew this change would not be to my liking.

I arrived back in Frankfurt late at night and went straight to my apartment. The next day was Sunday, and I could sleep in. The telephone rang early. It was a member of the consulate family who was calling me to tell me of the accidental death of our beloved consul general.

Chapter 7

I immediately got out of bed and went to the consulate in Frankfort, Germany, when the consulate family got the news— our beloved consul general had been killed in an automobile accident on the German Autobahn, a super highway with no speed limit. They said he was killed instantly. It was going to be especially hard on his young daughter. When they were together, the rest of the world did not exist. Father and daughter: a loss that she would have to live with. His voice said, *She will deal with her loss as all of you will deal with your losses.*

For some reason, the consul general, it seemed to me, had always taken a special interest in me. He had told me he would ensure that my next assignment would include training so that I would be prepared to take on more responsibilities and, of course, get promoted. With his death, I was again running with the pack without his help, no special treatment. Again his voice said, *Now you have to deal with change that you have not planned on.* I understood. I was thinking more and more about resigning from the Department of State Foreign Service and rejoining the Army. In my opinion and from what I knew at the time, if the Army said something, they would follow through. I learned later this was not necessarily true. His voice said, *Deal with change and do what you want to do. Stay in harmony with your soul.* I resigned and headed home to Georgia.

My mother liked getting letters from me with the Department of State's return address on them. She would have preferred I kept working for the Department of State. My father said, "Just do your best." I had informed both of them that I was going to rejoin the

Army and apply for OCS. They were both supportive and said, "If that's what you want to do." Dad said, "You know Vietnam is going on." I did. I rejoined the Army and was shipped to Fort Benning, Georgia, for BT. This time around, it was a lot of fun. I was in good physical shape and, because of my prior service, knew the difference between those things that were important and those things not to sweat. I was appointed Platoon or PLT guide probably because of my age since I was the oldest in the PLT and my prior service. Our PLT took most of the awards given for excellent training, just like the first time I went through BCT at Fort Knox, Kentucky, with the college guys leading the way. But now it was my job. We were all doing our best, and it paid off.

We were getting "at-a-boys" from everyone, including the cadre. I applied for OCS during this period and was selected for artillery OCS at Fort Sill, Oklahoma. While undergoing the pre-OCS training, the attack on the President of Korea and his wife and Korea's priority request for additional troop support from the Korean government to our government cut our plans to attend OCS. We all had MOS's by this time, and based on the need to meet field units manning requirements in Korea, we were all shipped to Korea. So much for OCS, or so we thought. Some of us were not displeased. Korea was better than Vietnam, and we all expected to be going there, living with change. As we were being processed into Korea, the commanding general came in to give his welcome speech and asked, "Does anyone have any questions?" I was not brave enough to stand up and ask, but one OCS selectee was. He asked the general when the soldiers selected to attend OCS would be going back to the United States to attend the training. The general turned to his aide and said, "What is he talking about?" The aide answered, "I don't know." The general then asked, "How many OCS-approved selectees are out there?" At least one hundred soldiers stood. He turned to the aide and said angrily, "Find out what the heck is going on and get those soldiers an answer. Do I make myself clear?" The aide replied, "Yes, sir!" He then turned to us and said, "Captain Lee will get you an answer. He is in charge of getting you back to attend OCS. Are there any more questions?" No one said anything. "Good. Have a good tour in Korea. If Captain Lee does his job right, it may be a short one for some of you."

We were called to attention, and the general walked out. Captain Lee was left standing at the podium. Before we were all dismissed, he instructed all the OCS-approved candidates to stand fast. There were well over a hundred soldiers left. He had a roster of all the soldiers who had been in attendance. He said, "I'm going to read off the names on this roster. If you hear your name, please sound off." The process went quickly, and when he had finished, he said, "Get out a piece of paper and write down my name and phone number. When you get to your unit, please inform the personnel officer that you are an OCS selectee. Also, tell him I'm working on instructors on getting guidance from the Department of the Army as to what action we are to take. I will call you as soon as I get guidance from DA. Are there any more questions?" No one said anything. "Thank you. I will stay in touch with each of you until this is resolved. That is all." With that, we continued to process for our assignments in Korea.

The next day, we were shipped to our new assignments. I was assigned to an artillery unit in the Fire Direction Control Center or FDCC, a good job, and the unit was filled with good guys who welcomed me in and made me feel I belonged. I was lucky…again. Everything was going well for me in my new unit. The guys all got along well, but I noticed a few with good tans. While we were at the club drinking one night, I asked one of them, "How did you get that good tan?"

He said, "Look over at SP4 Rogers and PFC Smith. They both have good tans, don't they?"

I said, "They sure do! How?"

Specialist Brickridge, Brick for short, said, "We all came here from Vietnam."

"How did that happen?"

"You remember when the North Koreans tried to kill the South Korean president and his wife? Well, it seemed he had the pull with the United States to beef up the strength of the American units here in Korea."

"What about Vietnam?"

Brick said, "I guess that just shows you which country is the most important to the United States, or at least which has the most political pull." He continued, "The cold here beats getting shot at. I'm one happy dude to get out of Vietnam alive. Let's talk about something else." And with that, the conversation about Vietnam was over.

The next day, I received a call from Captain Lee. He wanted to know if I could clear my unit and leave for Seoul, Korea, to be shipped back to the United States on Saturday to attend Infantry OCS one week later. I said, "I will have my bags packed and ready to go." He said, "Your orders have been hand-carried to your unit. I thought that would be your answer. Report to your company commander. He will have someone assist you in clearing your unit and provide your transportation here." I thanked Captain Lee for his help, and he said, "Good luck in OCS. Maybe we will meet again when you are an officer, and you can buy me a drink." I said, "That's a drink I will be glad to buy. Again, thanks." He hung up, and I went to report to the company headquarters.

The first sergeant was waiting on me with my clearance papers, and Brick was standing with him to help me clear the unit. I then noticed that both of them had good tans. The first sergeant said, "Specialist Brickridge will help you clear. I have initialed most of the places you would normally have to clear, but you have not been here long enough to use most of them. Brick will take you around to expedite your clearance." I could not help but notice the bond between them, and the first sergeant never called anyone else by his nickname. Brick looked at me and said, "Let's go," and away we went in the first sergeant's jeep. Brick looked at me and said, "You seem like a good guy. Do you know what you are in for?" I said, "Not for real." He said, "You are going to be an infantry lieutenant in Vietnam in a few short months. Listen to your men, talk to them, but most important, never think you are too good to do things you ask them to do. Don't be afraid to lead, but lead with your head and heart. Do those things, and you may live to come home, or more importantly, the men you lead will live to come home. I wish you well, and I'm still glad to be out of that hell."

Brick and I cleared the unit in record time, and Brick handed the clearance papers to the first sergeant, who signed them and said, "Here is your copy, and good luck. Brick," again with the nickname, "fill him in on Vietnam as you drive him to Seoul." The first sergeant looked at me again and said, "Take care of your men, and they will take care of you. Good luck." With that, we drove up to my barracks and picked up my duffel bag. We were off to Seoul, where I would fly out the next day for the good old USA. The flight was a commercial flight, which was mixed with civilians and soldiers. The soldiers were all in high spirits. They were going home and would be closing out this chapter of their lives. His voice said, *Look around you. See the joy of change, but look closely, and you will see something else. The acceptance of change is not always joy. Remember, in the days and months ahead, change is not always joy. Big changes are headed your way.*

Up to this point in my life, change had always brought another adventure, something to look forward to; life had been good to me. But as I looked more closely at some of the tanned faces around me, I could see in their faces the hurt, loneliness, and other lines of concern and worry that I could not know or understand. The flight went on, and we landed in San Francisco. In short order, I was on a plane to Atlanta, Georgia. I slept most of the way, even though it was daylight; changing time zones mess up your biological clock. I arrived in Atlanta where my brother met me and drove me home. I had just enough time to buy a car and say hello to everyone before I was off to Infantry OCS. A new chapter in my life was about to begin.

I reported to OCS on Sunday, just like the last time. The only thing that had changed at OCS was the buildings we, our class, were assigned. I reported in, and the harassment started, but this time it

HINSTON ROBINSON

did not seem to bother me. I had changed; OCS had not. The way to make junior officers was to put the pressure on and see how we as candidates could take it. I was still in good physical shape from basic training, and my mental attitude was in as good a shape as my physical shape. OCS was, in fact, going to be fun, so no quitting this time. The OCS weeks flew by, and before we knew what was happening, it was graduation day. I called and invited my parents to come to the graduation. Dad said he did not know if they could make it. He said they both wanted to come. That was the end of the conversation—they would come if they could.

I was on stage with the other candidates when I heard a very familiar cough. It was my dad. I knew that my parents had made it to see me get commissioned in the Army of the United States. It was a proud day for me and, I think, one for them. Somehow time was limited for them, and all they had time to say was how much seeing me graduate meant to them. Then they were on their way back home. I was given a week's leave before reporting to Fort Polk, Louisiana, for my first duty assignment. It was over before it started good. I said good-bye to friends and family, and I was off to be a training officer in an infantry, Advanced Individual Training or AIT unit. The cycle of eight weeks was about halfway through when I reported. The soldiers were being well-trained and were very proud of themselves. It was a joy to watch them train and interact with each other. I soon connected the dots. I was them, ten years earlier.

As their training was coming to an end and each soldier was receiving orders, a large number was headed for Vietnam. The ones that received orders to other places seemed disappointed. Brick's words played in my head: "I'm glad to be out of that hell." I did not ask him, but he wore a combat infantryman badge with a wreath, and the quiet calmness that came over him spoke louder than words. There was a place that you did not go. I remembered the night in the bar when he said, "Let's talk about something else." We did. I wondered if these young men knew what they were getting into. Brick's question to me: "Do you know what you are in for?" My answer was,

"Not for real." I knew then that these young soldiers did not have a clue as to what they were in for. I knew in a few short months, I would be joining them. Somehow the clarity of what was to come almost made me sick.

I went through two or three more cycles of AIT. They never changed, but I had changed. I tried to follow Brick and the first sergeant's advice, which, coupled with leadership principles taught in OCS, seemed to work when followed. It was easier to talk a good game than to follow Brick and the first sergeant's advice not to expect more from the men than I was willing to give to them. I tried to follow their advice, though. Out of each cycle of soldiers, some would ask, "When are you going to Vietnam, Lieutenant?" The "I don't know" came easily, but the nagging question in my soul was, "When are you going to Vietnam and be a part of the soldiers you are training?"

The same question was playing in the minds of two of the other training officers. We were at the club one night, and over too many beers, it was decided the right thing to do was to volunteer for Vietnam. We knew it was only a matter of time before we received orders for Vietnam, anyway. So the next day, all three of us went in to see the Company Commander and volunteer. His concern was how it would make him look if three of his officers wanted to volunteer at the same time. That only confirmed what we thought about him. He was out for number one: himself. We agreed—odd man out gets to volunteer first, so we flipped a coin. Boy, what luck, I was odd man out, and my volunteer papers for Vietnam went in that day. Until I received my orders, when asked by soldiers whom I was training when I was going to Vietnam, I would say, "Just as soon as I get orders. You don't think I would let you fight this war without me, do you? I will be there to keep you out of trouble and save your asses if I have to." I knew that was a bunch of bullshit, and I suspect they did too, but it gave us a chance to laugh together.

At that time, the road ahead was not full of death and young bodies that would never heal. Vietnam, here I come.

Chapter 8

Vietnam was waiting as I went home to Bowden, Georgia, for a short two weeks. I decided to drive to Travis Air Force Base, California, for a flight to Vietnam. A family member agreed to fly to California to pick up my car and drive it back to Georgia. The trip across America was beautiful. I stopped at several tourist hot spots, but I must admit the most awesome was the Grand Canyon. His voice said, *See the work I have done. Rejoice. For through you, your heart, and your mind, I feel the same joy you feel. When you are awestruck, I am awestruck. When you see beauty, I see beauty. As I walk with you, beside you, your feelings are mine also. I will always be with you.*

The trip was over before I knew it. I gave the keys to my niece, and I took a cab to Travis Air Force Base to catch a plane to Vietnam. I thought we soldiers would all ride on an Air Force plane for the flight, but no, we were herded out the door to this beautiful Air America jet. What a surprise. As we boarded the plane, it even smelled good and new. We were all seated when the stewardess, one of several, asked for our attention. She welcomed us aboard and instructed us to fasten our seatbelts, as we would be taking off in just a few minutes. The plane was already taxiing for takeoff. We were at the end of the runway when the rumble and high pitch of the engines left no doubt we would soon be airborne. The power of the engines pressed us against the back of our seats. As I was seated by a window, I could see the ground below disappearing, and at that moment, it became real that I was headed to Vietnam to be in a war. It took just a few minutes before the plane leveled off, and another stewardess was on the speaker. She again welcomed us aboard and informed us that they would be serving a meal in just a few minutes.

The plane was full of soldiers, with just a few people dressed in civilian clothes. Judging from their haircuts and some with a fair degree of facial hair, they were probably civilians. They said little or nothing to their fellow passengers. The flight also had some NCOs who sported CIBs with a wreath. This was a surefire sign that they had been to Vietnam before. They also said little and just watched as the "virgins," as I later learned they called those of us who had never been to Vietnam, seemed to be having a good time. We had not been touched by war. The stewardess came around with our food. It was a good steak with all the trimmings.

"This is the way to go to a war," was the comment from the virgin crowd. The true warriors said nothing, just giving us blank stares. Their looks should have told us something bad was just a few days/hours away, but they said nothing, and our lighthearted mood continued. In a few hours, the plane had become quiet. I let my seat go back as far as it would go and was sound asleep in just a minute. I awoke with a shudder, or thought I was awake. His voice said, *Change is coming. You will see and experience a side of my totality that you have never experienced. As of today, you have seen beauty, experienced joy, made friends, and felt safe and loved. These have made you what you are today. The few negatives in your life have been short and mostly forgotten, but what is ahead will change you forever. Remember, I will always be with you. Now go back to sleep.* The warm feeling I had felt in the past came over me, and I was asleep. The next thing I heard was the sweet voice of the stewardess saying, "Please fasten your seatbelts. We will be landing in Saigon in just a few minutes." The plane seemed to drop out of the air. The engines reversed their pitch, and we felt the strong G-force on our bodies. One of the virgins said, "I could land this plane better and smoother than that." One of the warriors looked at him and said, "Come in slow and low, and Charlie will blow your ass out of the sky. Give me the rough landings every time." With his comment, a number of the warriors laughed, and one said, "That is your first lesson, newbie."

We grabbed our bags and unloaded the plane in record time. There was a crew already checking and cleaning the plane, and a fueling truck was standing by to refuel the plane. It would leave in short order with a group of soldiers going home. A bus pulled up with a new crew for the plane. The old crew got on the bus, and as we were herded into a waiting area, we could see the soldiers getting ready to leave. Some had bandages covering what must have been wounds. Others looked at us with a strange stare. No one said anything. Then we were rushed into a large building. Teams of assignment personnel were waiting. They called out our names and told us where to go. The buses outside were marked with major units. You got on the one that was to be your unit or home for the next year.

My assignment before leaving Fort Polk, Louisiana, was to Military Advisory Command Vietnam or MACV. Some old soldiers, the warriors, had told me that orders got changed all the time and not to get too locked in on my orders. So far, at least, my orders were good. I was told to get on the MACV bus. I asked one of the assignment officers what MACV did. He said, "They will tell you when you get to your unit. Now get on the bus." A number of us were loaded on the bus, and away we went. It seemed like a short ride when we pulled up to this large building. We were instructed to secure all our belongings, get off the bus, and go through the double doors, which were just then being swung open for us to enter. We walked into this large room with several tables. A major was standing in front of the room. He asked us to be seated, and for the first time, I noticed there were soldiers of all grades and ranks within the group.

The major said, "We will now start you in-country briefing. For those of you who have not been to Vietnam, all of what we say will be new to you. Those who have been here before may think that what we are saying is a bunch of bulls—t, but let me assure you what you are going to hear and the training you will receive in the next two weeks is key not only to your survival but to the survival of the teams that you will become a part of. The effectiveness of your role as an advisor will also be determined by how well you incorporate the tried and proven concepts you will be taught. Now for those of you wondering what I'm going to be doing, let me give you a little background before I answer that question.

"Special Forces, as they were trained to do, were very effective in motivating Vietnamese communities to maintain their soldiers and worked beside them in securing their areas of operations or AOs. MACV, using their methods, has formed advisor teams to live, work, train, supply, support operations, and do what is necessary in ensuring your assigned unit's success in supporting their communities. Depending on where you are assigned and what level of command you are assigned to advise will determine the number of soldiers on your team. I can't help but notice we have several first and second lieutenants among you. I can almost assure you that you will be assigned to MACV teams. These are generally five-man teams advising companies or smaller Vietnamese units and communities.

"I would suggest strongly that you pay special attention to the dos and don'ts when living with the Vietnamese. Now, the first thing you will do is stow your clothing and equipment and then be assigned a place to bunk down for the next two weeks. The class schedule will be posted in your bunk area. There will be no excuses for not attending classes. This room is your classroom. When you come to class tomorrow, there will be your name and future unit (team of assignment) posted. Please do not change your seating arrangement. The reason for this will become clear as we start your training. After you stow your equipment and get your bunk assignment, you are free for the rest of the day. You are not to leave this compound. Are there any questions?" There were none.

The next morning started with a bang, literally. It sounded like a gun going off right next to your bed. That was all we needed to get out of bed and get into our new jungle fatigues, jungle boots, and jungle hats to go eat chow. The chow was unbelievable: every kind of fruit, meat, eggs; you name it, it was there for the taking. I learned that the cooks and the mess sergeant took great pride in feeding the troops. What a morale boost that must have been for the units. I learned later of the generosity of some of the mess sergeants. They kept our MACV team supplied with food out of their willingness to give and share. But I'm getting ahead of myself. I had not even been assigned to a unit or team yet.

We walked into the classroom and, as instructed, found our table with our name and team of assignment. I noticed at the back of the room there were several soldiers standing around. They all looked at us as if they were inspecting us. Then the major from the day before went to the front of the room. He had also been standing at the back of the room and again asked for our attention. He said, "It is my pleasure to introduce you to some of the team members you will be joining in two weeks when you leave here." He called off team assignments and names and asked if we would stand up and be recognized. He called out several names before I heard him say, "Second Lieutenant Robinson." I stood up, and I saw this skinny first lieutenant or LT and a master sergeant or MSG heading toward me. Both of them looked meaner than hell. As they approached me, neither said a word. I just stood there as both of them walked around me.

Finally, the lieutenant said, "Do you think he is a keeper?"

The master sergeant said, "From the looks of this crowd, we could do worse."

"I agree," said the lieutenant. With that, his hand went out, and he said, "Welcome to MACV Team forty-nine, the best damn team in Vietnam." The master sergeant looked at me in the eye for a minute and said, "Welcome to our team." Then the lieutenant said, "Listen to their advice, and we will have our own training program when you join us in two weeks. No bull, this is serious business if you have not figured that out yet. You will when Charlie tries to kill your ass. We have a good MACV team. You will fit into our team well. I'm looking forward to you joining our team. How did you like our introduction? We practiced that routine so that we could see how much training we had to give you before we let you get shot at. You passed with flying colors. We will pick you up in two weeks. See you. By the way, I'm LT First. Call me LT F." And with that, they were gone.

The training started in with another welcome to Vietnam. The welcome was short and to the point. The LTC said, "You are here for one purpose and only one purpose—to win the war. If you think this is some kind of vacation, get that out of your minds now. Some of you who are returning after one or more tours here may think that being assigned to MACV as an advisor is a piece of cake. Well, let me dispel that idea right now. Last week, for the numbers assigned, MACV had the highest number of casualties of any American unit in Vietnam. So, for those of you who have been here before and the virgins, pay attention in class. What you learn here could just save your life and the lives of those of your team or the Vietnamese you advise."

We went over the history of Vietnam and discussed the different ethnic groups, and after that class, I wondered how they even lived together. It seemed each group had its own objective and was only helping military forces that supported its agenda. Several other countries had sent their military and some civilian support elements to support in the war effort. The country was divided into areas of operations, and of course, the United States had taken the largest share. But on occasion, responsibilities overlapped. We were instructed how to resolve these issues. The instructor said, "Your problems may come up when you draw up your fire support plans to cover your ground operations. A bigger problem may be if you are in a firefight and need fire support immediately. We have had some problems in this area."

One of us, also an LT, stood up and asked, "What kind of fire support can we expect?" The instructor said, "That is a good question. I see that you have been here before with American pure or American-based units in charge. Fire support has been less of a problem. This is because American units plan fire support for most of their operations and generally don't have to consider other forces in their AOs. You, on the other hand, will be advising Vietnamese units, and even when you are on a joint operation with an American unit, you will still need to know how to get fire support. LT, you asked what fire support was available. Now I will try to answer that question. Naval guns can hit any grid square in Vietnam. Properly planned, this can be a lifesaver, and the Air Force and the Army both provide air support fire. This is a key planning factor. All American and other forces, including the Vietnamese, have ground support, artillery, and mortar support. That about covers the fire support you can get if properly planned and if you know contacts and how to reach them. Fire support is a lifesaver. Do I have any more questions on the subject?" There were no more questions.

Chapter 9

The advisor training was going well. I noticed that one or two soldiers had left the group. It was rumored they were not suitable to be advisors. I wondered what made a soldier suitable or unsuitable to become an advisor. We discussed this among ourselves but had not heard a word from the training staff at the school. We discussed with school cadre the history of Vietnam and how the Vietnamese people had been subjected to some very difficult and brutal times by different foreign powers. It was acknowledged that some Vietnamese thought the United States had some thoughts about replacing the French as the power to again control Vietnam. The Vietnamese had paid a high price in defeating the French at Dien Bien Phu. They did not want another foreign power taking the place of the French. The instructors said to just be aware of very different views on how the Vietnamese believe the best course of action was for them to become a democracy and govern themselves.

We had been in classes for a week. The subjects ranged from communications, fire support, all kinds of weapons, ranks of village leaders, respect for our host country, Vietnam, Vietnamese manners, treatment of women and children, the hands-off rule of sexual conduct within your area of responsibility—you name it, we discussed the subject. In all, the courses were enjoyable and informative. On Sunday, the last thing the instructors said before dismissing us for the rest of the day was, "We have a special treat for Monday." With that, they said, "Have a good night."

We were getting used to having a twelve-hour day. Sundays of eight hours were a treat. We could go to the PX and shop. The PX was like a department store, except on Long Binh Supply Depot, otherwise known as little Saigon. The PX there was more like a very big department store, like in the States. This would be my second time to go. The number of American civilians shopping I had seen there the first time I had gone had been a surprise. The second time, I was in for a bigger surprise. There were hundreds of civilians shopping. Where did they come from? What did they do? I went to the snack bar and ordered a hamburger and Coke. You could get anything, all kinds of food. My order was waiting for me at the cash register. I found a table and sat down to eat.

No sooner had I sat down when this young lady asked if she could join me. I was delighted to have company. I introduced myself, she introduced herself, and we began talking. I told her how surprised I was with all the American civilians there, and I wondered what they were doing. She looked at me kind of funny, and then she laughed. "I knew you had not been in country long when I asked to join you. But just a week! You have a lot to learn about what is going on. I teach school here, both Vietnamese and Americans, with a few other countries' children thrown in, making up my class. You see, some Americans and other countries, depending on their status, have their families living here. So, I got a job as a teacher."

"How many of you are here?"

"I'm sure if you counted them all, there would be several hundred." I could now appreciate the concern of the Vietnamese and that maybe another foreign power just wanted to take control of their country. We discussed living in Vietnam. She enjoyed the food and loved the people and the travel. Saigon was a great place to live, at least, there where she was. She looked at her watch and said she had to run. Monday was a workday. No seven twenty-four-hour days for her. The instructors had made the point: we would be on duty 24-7 when we were at our duty assignments. Then they followed this up by saying, "Of course, you will get a break about halfway through your twelve-month tour of duty. Be thinking about where you would like to go." I later learned this was called Rest and Relaxation or

R&R. It had proven to reduce battle fatigue. It was a cheap way to keep soldiers with experience in the field fighting.

Monday came quickly and early. I could have slept all day. There were two buses parked outside, and all the cadre at the school were waiting. We had instructions from the cadre to load up. We climbed on board, and away we went. A cadre informed us we would be going to a typical Vietnamese village where we would visit the people, like the village elders and the defenders called the regional or popular forces [RF or PF], and look over village security setups, and finally have lunch with the village chief and his guests. This would include most of the village. "Be aware. Today you are not in an advisor role. You are a guest. I hope you enjoy the day, but be aware. This is not your hometown USA. The food will be prepared and served buffet-style. Eat as much as you want, but if you take something, you are expected to eat it. Their communal meal you will be served is an important part of the culture of Vietnam. Failure to eat and share in these meals will affect your ability to advise and assist their communities. If any of you feel you cannot or will not fully support the communal meal, please let one of the cadre know now." No one spoke. "All right, no one has copped out, so we will be arriving at our guest village shortly. The following soldiers will get off here with Captain Eldin."

I noticed a Vietnamese man seated beside him who had not been in any of our classes. Captain Eldin stood up and said, "Let me introduce you to Sergeant Yen. He will be our interpreter for today. He is a member of the village PF and speaks excellent English. You may ask him any questions about the village and its citizens. Do you have any questions?" No. "Good."

The bus was slowing down, it pulled off the side of the highway, and we were instructed to get off. There was no village in sight. Captain Eldin and Sergeant Yen saw the expressions on our faces and laughed. Captain Eldin said, "I hope you enjoy a good walk." He said, "*Di voi toi.*" ("Follow me" in Vietnamese.) We had been instructed to leave our weapons at the school, but somehow, the captain and Sergeant Yen both had their M-16 rifles with them. Captain Eldin could see our concern and said to us, "In general terms, this is a secured area. The reason you do not or did not bring your weapons is that we had an incident where a just-in-country soldier became frightened and opened fire on some friendlies. Therefore, during this outing, only cadre carry weapons. It is only a short walk."

We first saw some straw or short bamboo pens with chickens in them. Then we noticed small houses, some built out of the same material as the fences with the chickens. Some had wooden floors, and some had clay floors. As we went into the center of the village, there were a few completely wooden structures, and at the center of the village, there stood a brick church. Captain Eldin said, "This is a typical Vietnamese village." The village chief came out of one of the larger wooden building to welcome us to his village. He spoke English very well, another surprise. Sergeant Yen said, "Don't be surprised. Many Vietnamese speak several languages, including English." We were then told by Captain Eldin, "You are free to visit people who live here."

The doors of the church opened, and an older gentleman began to speak before we scattered. He was also welcoming us to the village and indicated we should visit his church before we left. SGT Yen said, "He is our priest and does not speak English too well. When and if you want to meet him, I would be glad to be your interpreter. He has been our priest for a very long time. He has been with us here in Vietnam before the war. We love and respect him not only because he is our priest, but he is also our friend and a supporter through some very hard times. I request that you pay him your respects by visiting his church." With that, we scattered and went to visit the people.

We were not the first class of advisors to visit this village. We were welcomed into their homes, and each one wanted to give us a small gift, which they had made by hand. We had been instructed to take these gifts and express our thanks but give nothing in return. We were guests. Each house had tea waiting for us. Even though I was not a great tea drinker, with the very sweet milk they added, I soon learned to enjoy it. In fact, it was very good. It was time to go back to the center of the village where we would all meet to have lunch. Next to the church was a large covered area where a long table had been placed and was stacked with food.

The village chief, the village elders, and the priest were all there. The village chief asked how our visit had been, and then he said, "I thought I would like for you to share a meal with us." Captain Eldin and Sergeant Yen gave a customary bow, and the chief led us into the covered area for lunch. The food was delicious. Of course, I had developed a liking for heavily spiced foods in Korea. Even though I had been there only a short time, I had eaten at local Korean restaurants several times and had always enjoyed kimchi, a Korean national dish. I noticed everyone was paying attention to me while I was freely helping myself to the red hot sauce used as a dip for the lettuce leaves, which were filled with rice and meat. When I looked and felt embarrassed, all the Vietnamese began to smile.

Sergeant Yen said, "You are paying the village much respect by enjoying our food so much. Do not be embarrassed. Some Americans will not eat or do not like our food." I said to SGT Yen, "They don't know what they're missing." He laughed, turned to the village chief and the other VIPs, and said something in Vietnamese. They all laughed. The village chief then said, "I wish all of us and our American friends could enjoy our communal meals and get-togethers as we are enjoying this day." Then he passed a dish of something to me, and thank goodness, I had seen him spread it on some rice bread. I followed suit. The food in the dish had a strong taste of fish, garlic, and red pepper and was the consistency of warm butter. I took a good bite, and the taste was overwhelmingly good. I just took a chance and did a slight bow to the village chief and expressed how delicious the delicate taste on the bread was. He seemed very pleased and said something in Vietnamese to his guest. They all nodded their approval.

Sergeant Yen said, "There are not many Americans who eat and enjoy our food the way you seem to. This makes everyone very proud and happy to have you as a guest." We finished eating, and all the

Vietnamese left to take an after-lunch break or a short nap. They had told us of this custom in school. The priest invited us to see his church. We all followed him inside. It was a hot day on the outside, but inside the church, it was cool. He invited us to sit down and then started telling us about his arrival in Viet-Nam. It seems he was a young priest when he first came to their village, but after a few years, he became like their young father. Then, as he became older, they became dearer to him. He had asked to stay on in the first few years, and then the church fathers just stopped asking him if he wanted to leave, and so he stayed with his family. It had been a good life. You could see by his expressions the love he had for the place and its people. His voice said, "Only a few people are blessed to find his peace and love for his fellowman. In the months ahead, you will see and feel the horror of what man can do. Enjoy today these times. They will be short-lived."

Captain Eldin was shaking my shoulder and saying, "We have to go." He said, "You did us proud at lunch. You cannot imagine how much it means to the Vietnamese to have an American like their food. Good show." I said, "Good food." He laughed and said, "You are going to make a good advisor and a representative of our country." We then went outside and joined the others. Captain Eldin said, "I would like to show you a typical RF/PF compound." We walked a short distance out of the village, and on this rise was a triangular compound. We went up to the front gate, which was guarded by a Vietnamese SGT who spoke excellent English and introduced us to the captain (Dai Uy Thuyen Truong), who was in charge of the compound and several Vietnamese soldiers. The compound had gun emplacement on the three corners of the berm. The berm was about four or five feet high with barbed wire or razor wire that covered the top and sides and extended several feet from the berm. The only way to get in was through the gate.

Then Dai Uy said, "We close the gate at night and put up razor wire and, of course, claymore mines." These were directional mines that used an explosive called C-4. These mines, when exploded, formed a deadly fan in front of them. Inside the compound were several bunkers built into the berm. Captain Eldin said, "You may want to look inside one of these bunkers. For some of you, you will be living in one just like it." Then Dai Uy said, "Follow me," and we went to a steel Con-X container, a steel shipping crate, that had been sandbagged for a communications, command, and control bunker. Captain Eldin said, "These at other compounds have survived direct mortar hits. I would advise if your compound does not have one, get one." Someone said, "How?" Captain Eldin said, "Getting one will determine how resourceful you can be. Just kidding. A number of American units have extra ones, and the engineers can be or are willing to be conned into helping. Your other team members will know how to work with the American units in your area to build you almost anything. This bunker is just one example."

We spent an hour looking around and talking to the Vietnamese soldiers. I was very surprised at how many spoke excellent English. Captain Eldin said, "It is time for us to go." He thanked the Vietnamese captain and made a slight bow to the soldiers. Then we were out the gate and headed back to the village. He said, "In case you are wondering, those soldiers are local men who provide security to the village. They have been very effective in their mission. It kind of works this way. When intelligence or other information about VC activity comes to the attention of the central province government, a request to assign an MAT or a mobile advisor team to a village is generally made. Based upon the expected scope of activity, a MAT team and a Vietnamese soldier unit may be coupled with an American unit to conduct an operation and provide security to the village. You have been instructed about your role in these types of operations. It is essential in liaising with the American units you develop a fire support plan. You must know how and be able to communicate with these American units. Your team and the lives of the Vietnamese unit you are advising depend upon your ability to perform this task without fail. I know this has been covered time and time again, but your lives depend on it." Everyone looked sober. What we were in for was beginning to sink in.

We arrived back in the village, and we lined up to shake hands and bow to the village chief and his guest. The priest shook our hands and said, "May God be with you." We walked back to the main road, and just like clockwork, the bus arrived to take us back to the Long Binh supply depot compound. The major, a rank between a captain and a lieutenant colonel, who was in charge of the compound, said, "I hope you have enjoyed your day. But more importantly, I hope you have learned something."

The rest of the week was going over key subjects: history, tactics, fire support planning, liaisons with other units, both American, Vietnamese, and some cases other Allied forces, etc. We drew some more equipment. The equipment varied depending on where you were going and what you were assigned to do. Overall, it was just like any Army operation, but the school had it down to an art form.

LT F showed up at noon on Friday, just as he said he would. He asked me if I had learned anything, and I said, "I think so." He said, "Good. I also understand you like Vietnamese food, right?" Before I could answer, he added, "We will go to this Vietnamese place I know about. The food will curl your toes." He had a different SFC with him this time. He said to me, "Meet SFC Hoffman. He is our team medic, the best in Vietnam. Are you ready to get the hell out of this place and go meet your new family?" I said yes, turned to SFC Hoffman, and said, "I'm glad to meet you." He smiled and said, "Likewise," and with that, we were off. LT F had picked up my gear and threw it into a trailer his jeep was pulling. He said, "Now let's go rustle up some groceries. Pay attention, LT. This is how we feed ourselves." I noticed a number of bottles of whisky and other stuff in the box beside me. LT F said, "That's our trading stuff." We must have stopped at least six mess halls, and at each one, we came away with boxes of food stuff. We had steaks, hot dogs, pork chops, bacon, flour, powdered milk—you name it, we had boxes of it. We could have started our own grocery store.

LT F turned to SFC Hoffman and said, "Do you think this will keep us for a while?" SFC Hoffman said, "It's a good haul." I heard the in-charge soldiers at the mess hall asking for items, and LT F or SFC Hoffman would say, "We will have it next time." The soldiers at the mess halls did not wear rank on their cook whites, so I don't know what rank they were. A few mess sergeants in their jungle fatigues did the trading. They all seemed to want the whisky. The younger soldiers wanted VC clogs or sandals or anything that looked like it had belonged to the Viet Cong. We drove out of Saigon, and LT F said, "I want to be back in our compound safe and sound before dark. I don't want to get LT R shot today. It would be bad form." I guess LT R was going to be my name for the time being.

We drove into province headquarters about two hours before dark. LT F said, "Let's go meet the province senior advisor." He was a tall and large lieutenant colonel. LT F said, "Sir! I would like you to meet LT Robinson, our new Bravo. LT R, my new name again, did well in advisory school and is ready to go to work." The LT C turned to me and said, "I'm LT C Speirs. Welcome to our team." LT F then said, "Do you have anything else for us, sir?" The LTC looked at him and said, "No." LT F said, "I want to get back to my team before dark." LTC Speirs said, "I have nothing else for you at this time." With that, we both saluted and walked out. SFC Hoffman had given the province cook some of our groceries. "Good job, Hoffman," LT F said with a note of respect in his voice; they were true comrades. "We must keep them on our side." With that, we were back in the jeep and off to my new home and family.

We arrived just before sunset and drove into a compound much like the one I had visited on Monday. The team had a bunker near the center of the compound. I noticed it was a steel Con-X with sandbags filled and piled high over the whole structure. LT F walked inside and said, "Come into your new home. You have met our Master Sergeant Parker and SFC Hoffman. Now for our heavy weapons team advisor, please meet SFC Murphy. This is SGT Dot, our interpreter, and, of course, his lovely wife, who is also our cook. They are the best people in the world. People, I would now like you to meet our new Bravo, LT Robinson, whom I shall call LT R." I shook hands and bowed to SGT Dot's wife.

The questions began: "Where are you from in the world? Where did you go to school? You look old to be a lieutenant." I explained what had happened with my career. They gave their history, and after a while, LT F said, "I have had a very long day, and I'm going to bed." Beds were located around the walls with mosquito nets hung for privacy. Not much privacy there. The MSG said, "LT R, this is your bunk." It looked like I was going to be LT R whether I liked it or not. In fact, I did not mind. It sure beat the hell out of Hinston, which is my first name. I told the team I was kind of tired also and wanted to go to bed. They said okay.

The MSG asked, "Who has first radio watch?" I sat up in bed, swung my feet to the floor, and said, "If you tell me what I'm supposed to do, I will take my turn." The MSG said, "You can have a free night, LT R." I got up anyway and said, "I understand SFC Hoffman has the first watch. If he or no one objects, I will let him teach me the ropes." Everyone said, "Fine." SFC Hoffman explained that we were in constant communication with the command and control or C&C at province headquarters. Nothing happened until our shift ended at 01:00 hours when SFC Brown took over. I climbed into bed and was sound asleep in about one minute.

The next morning, we were up early, and LT F said, "Come on, I want to introduce you around." SGT Hoffman was already gone. LT F said he was treating some village kids and would be giving health classes to some of the village women later in the day. He said, "We will stop by later and see him. He is an important player in winning the hearts and minds of the local people." We stopped at this local hangout, or so it seemed, and LT F ordered us a bowl of soup and a cup of coffee. The soup was delicious, and the coffee was something else. It was so strong it was almost like honey in texture, but when they added this concentrated sweet milk mixture, it was out of this world.

LT F looked at me and said, "You do enjoy their food, don't you?" I said yes. He added, "By the way, you made some points with the team last night by staying up with SFC Hoffman. I knew when we first met, you would be a team player. I love this team, and I don't want anything to happen to any of them, and, of course, not to me." He laughed. "Now, I must tell you, LTC Speirs sometimes comes up with these operations that could get us killed. I support any operations that has been planned and coordinated, coupled with good supporting plans from our American units. They can and are lifesavers. Our team has already had a near-disaster. We will not have another one as long as I'm team leader. I'm telling you this because I'm due to leave Vietnam in less than three months. I don't want you to get this team killed. If you go on any operations, make sure province has done their part. The MACV standard operating procedures (SOPs) require that coordination and fire support plans need to be finalized before any operation is conducted. Now, in support of the PF, we advise you and a team member can go on limited operations without all this planning. What I'm saying is small operations in support of a village is okay. Just call up the C&C at province and tell them you will be going out with a PF unit and what you are going to do. They will generally give you the okay. We will meet the unit and its commander who protects this village later today. He has an excellent unit, and his men like him. I don't think he requires them to pony up any part of their pay to him. You will find that happens in certain units. It's not a way to win the loyalty of your soldiers."

We finished our meal and headed down the road. Then we met the local unit and the Captain, who was coming back from an ambush the night before. LT F and the captain greeted each other warmly, and LT F said to the captain, "I would like for you to meet LT R. He is our new Bravo."

The captain looked me over and said, "I'm Dai Uy Knew."

I said, "I'm Thuong Si Robinson, and I'm glad to meet you."

He smiled and said, "I'm looking forward to working with you. LT F and I work well together." I noticed he also called our lieutenant LT F. We walked back to the restaurant from which we had just left. The soldier's food and the Dai Uy's food were served first. LT F told him we had just eaten, but we would have a cup of coffee. I was glad. The stuff was delicious. The Dai Uy and LT F discussed operations that we could assist and what kind of supplies they needed. I was learning my job firsthand. LT F was a professional officer, and you could see and feel the respect he garnered not only from the captain but also from the Vietnamese soldiers. I was lucky to have him as my team leader. I did not know how lucky I was until a few days later.

I went to the village with SFC Hoffman, and we got to talking about LT F. He said, "Don't say anything about it because he gets upset if anyone brings it up, but he is a Silver Star recipient from the Big Red One. He does not have to prove anything to anyone." Now I understood why he was treated with respect. He had earned it. We walked and rode over the area that we were assigned to assist and advise. The people seemed to welcome our presence. LT F said, "Don't be taken in by their attitude. They have been through a lot and are masters of pretension. I guess when you have to live under the yoke of a master or several masters, you learn to pretend if you want to survive."

We were back in the village. We had not met the village chief, but that was about to change. Coming down the main road was this distinguished-looking man with five or six other men in tow. LT F walked up to him and made a slight bow, which was returned by all of them. Then LT F put out his hand to shake hands, and the village chief did likewise. Again, the village chief spoke excellent English. He had a number of things he wanted LT F's help in getting. I soon learned he wanted the Americans to buy these things. LT F said, "I will see what is available." One of the key items was the razor wire, which the village chief said was needed to improve the security of the hamlets or very small villages in the area. LT F said okay. Then he turned to me and said, "I would like you to meet LT R." I made the customary bow and put out my hand, which was taken in a firm grip. He was letting me know he was in charge. He then said, "I understand you like our food very much." I said, "I do." Then he said, "We will have a village get-together with food for all to welcome you to our village."

When we left, I asked LT F how he knew that I liked Vietnamese food. LT F laughed. "Lesson number-whatever-is, you can't do anything without everyone knowing about it. So, be careful about what you say and do. Word travels fast here. It's better than our telephone party lines in the States. You did not have a private phone when you were growing up in Georgia, did you?" I said, "No. In fact, we just had a phone installed, and it's a party line."

"Well, you know what I mean. I think our phone back home had four people who could and would listen in on your conversation. Me and a few of my buddies, which included girls, would get on the phone and burn off the ears of some of the old ladies that listened in. The girls would go on about what we did the night before, and I must admit, some of the things they came up with were hard to imagine. But the looks we got when we went to church on Sunday could turn you to stone or maybe salt. Our parents said little to us about the pranks. I think they thought, 'This is what they get for listening in on other peoples' conversations.' You see, in the farmlands of Wisconsin, we believe in privacy. Those were the good old days. Three of my buddies have been killed here." With that, the conversation ended.

In just a week, I could tell when the talking ended. This was one of those times. That night, he and I went on an ambush with the PF company. Captain Knew was in high spirits, and his company was doing everything you expected of a well-trained and disciplined unit. LT F said he liked going on operations with Captain Knew and his company. He said they could handle any local VC units. The only problem was when a regular North Vietnamese unit coupled with a local VC unit came through. He said, "You had better done your homework." He meant planning and coordination. Sometime after midnight, all hell broke loose and just as quickly stopped. LT F said, "They probably killed a water buffalo. If so, we will have to pay for it. Of course, we will eat it at your welcome dinner." He smiled. Every day I thanked my seven stars I had gotten LT F for my leader in Vietnam. I had to learn fast because his time was getting shorter by the day, and he would be flying home in less than three months now.

Chapter 10

The team continued to go on operations with the local PF or RF. The rapport LT F had established with the Vietnamese soldiers and their officers was graciously being transferred to me by his leadership. He would often say to them, "LT R got you this," or "He will get you that." He would then take me with him to the many sources of supplies he had. He would always introduce me to the American units in our area of responsibility, and they all seemed to know him. The civilian units (LT F said, "Don't ask who they are or what they do") I suspected were from our Central Intelligence Agency (CIA) and could also come up with some hard-to-get items.

Some of the men would joke with LT F and say, "We will have you back over here a month after you go home." LT F would laugh and say, "When I get home to Mommy (meaning his wife), you don't have enough money in that little black box to get me to come back." They would all have a good laugh and either give him what we came for or tell him to see so and so for it. It was going to be hard to fill his shoes. One morning, about two or three o'clock, the radio traffic became intense. An RF unit in our area was in contact. The whole team was awake, and Sergeant Dot was interpreting the action for us. LT F said, "Those are CPT Knew's men. They will stand their ground." It seemed like the firefight went on for a few hours, but in reality the fighting lasted only about an hour. But as I later learned, an hour can be a lifetime.

We received a call from province headquarters instructing us to be at the firefight location the next morning, and ten o'clock would be a good time. LT F said, "It is showtime." LT F, SFC Hoffman, Sergeant Dot, and I left our position the next morning to arrive at ten o'clock as instructed. There was already a crowd. LTC Speirs was there with several officers and one senior NCO. The Vietnamese had a troop of VIPs. Among them was the province senior officer, which explained why LTC Speirs was there. I figured that out without the help of LT F or SFC Brown. LT F said, "Come on," and we walked over to where six bodies were laid out in a neat row. Two of the soldiers had their helmets covering their faces. I started to say something, but LT F cut me off and said, "I will tell you later."

CPT Knew was there. The senior province officer (SPO) and LTC Speirs all had their pictures taken, which included the dead soldiers, a mixture of North Viet Cong (NVA) and local Viet Cong (VC). The only differences were the uniforms. The first two in the row had on uniforms that matched, and the others had on some parts of uniforms but mostly clothes that were worn by all Vietnamese. We stood around while everyone talked and congratulated the Regional Forces (RF) lieutenant on his success. The SPO presented the lieutenant with a medal—again, more pictures. Then the show was over. The SPO and his staff were getting into their jeeps, and away they went.

LTC Speirs came over to us and instructed LT F to see what the local RF company needed and then what to get for them. With those instructions, he and his staff were in jeeps and headed back to Xuân Lôc Province headquarters for their air-conditioned offices. LT F's only comment was, "What an ass." CPT Knew came up, and LT F and he had a discussion on what the village needed and how we could help. CPT Knew asked LT F if we, the team, could spend the night there. He said it would help calm the village down. LT F said, "Sure." He then turned to me and said for all to hear, "LT R looks like he needs a bowl of the excellent Vietnamese soup that you serve here." There was a general sigh of relief, everyone from the village smiled, and off we went to get soup.

As we were eating, LT F told CPT Knew that he would drive back to our area and get some of the supplies they needed and return that afternoon. CPT Knew said that sounded good to him. We finished our soup, and as we got into our jeep, CPT Knew said, "I will see you this afternoon." LT F said, "He is just letting the village know that we will be back this afternoon." We headed back to our compound, and LT F turned to me and said, "You know, earlier I said I would tell you later." I said, "Yes, what was that all about?" He said, "You noticed the two soldiers with their helmets covering their faces?" I said yes. He then informed me that they were members of the RF unit and not VC. The show was on: the more VC you killed, the more money and supplies you were provided.

The province government would use the firefight to show they were aggressively routing out the VC. The story would bubble all the way to the top. The family of the local RF soldiers would be paid a king's ransom by their standards for their part in the "play" or war. "Everyone wins except the six dead soldiers," he said. He then looked at me with a chilling stare and said, "Don't let that happen to you or any of our team, okay?" We rode in silence for a few miles, and then he was back with us. SFC Hoffman told me later, "When he gets like that, leave him to himself. He will get over it." While we were riding in silence, I could not help but think about the soldiers we had just seen; all were very young. I had never seen a young person, my age or younger, dead before. Death did not happen to us; it was for old people. Those six young soldiers, I knew then, were only the beginning of what was to come.

We returned to our compound and loaded a trailer full of ammunition and some rolls of razor wire, wire that had very sharp flat barbs woven into it, and we carried enough food to feed the village for a week. LT F said, "This is one reason we get so much food when we go to Long Binh (Saigon). It is a good way to develop a supporting relationship with the village. If it was not, at least, marginally safe for our team to spend the next few days in their village, a villager would have told CPT Knew. Some village people know the local VC and inform CPT Knew about their activities. This village will be quiet for a few months. Then the show will repeat itself. One of the many things you have to be aware of is if the local people or the commander of a Vietnamese unit does not want you to go on an operation, it's probably best not to go. That's number one. Number two is sometimes the NVA come through here with large and small units, and the locals know nothing about the NVA operations. These are hard-hitting professionally led units that can and will spoil your day. You underestimate their fighting skills or their dedication, and you will lose and get yourself and the team killed. Don't let that happen."

Our team continued to go on operations with the local RF and PF. We managed to capture one NVA soldier who had come home to visit his family. I thought soldiers were the same the world over—they would come home to their friends and family. My mind went back to the six soldiers I had seen, which now seemed so long ago. LT F's time was getting short. He had less than a month before boarding a "freedom bird" or plane and flying home. LTC Speirs offered to let him come to the province headquarters until he flew out. He declined and said, "I will stay with my team. LT R and the team will take me to Saigon to fly home." LTC Speirs said okay. As we were leaving, a new first lieutenant was getting out of a jeep. LT F went over and introduced himself, Sergeant Dot, and me. They talked a few minutes, and LT F said, "Don't go on any operations that you don't have a fire support plan and coordination made with your supporting units. LTC Speirs sometimes does not do this right." The lieutenant looked at LT F and said, "We are here to fight, right?" LT F said, "Yes, but not to get yourself or your team killed." The lieutenant turned and walked away without saying another word. LT F said, "Maybe he will be lucky and survive long enough to learn."

Three days later, late at night, our radioman made contact with Gia Ray Mountain, a hot spot for NVA units coming and going north. It was not long before we heard the RF and the advisor team had suffered casualties. LT F said he was not lucky. The next day, we drove over to Gia Ray Mountain. This time, there were no VIPs and no one to take pictures. CPT Knew had lost several soldiers, and the advisor team had lost their leader, and one of the senior NCOs was wounded badly. If an advisor or American soldier was killed, that was a black mark against the local RF commander and the village in general. CPT Knew was upset. He told LT F that he advised the lieutenant not to go on the operation. He and the lieutenant had words, and CPT Knew agreed to go on the operation. CPT Knew selected and set up an ambush, but the lieutenant moved his team and a platoon of RF soldiers after being advised not to, and they were ambushed themselves. There was not a supporting fire plan.

It took several minutes to get clearance and support. CPT Knew said if it had not been for the gunships or helicopters equipped with several weapon systems that could and did clear large areas of anything living, his company and the advisor team would have all been killed. There was not one NVA soldier among the dead. Of course, the NVA, if possible, always carried their dead soldiers back with them. I do not know the reason for this unless they did not want them to be used or seen as dead NVA soldiers, part of the show. LT F was leaving the next week. He seemed to be distracted, and we all thought it was because he was going home. LT F got up one morning and said to me, "Get ready. We are going to see LTC Speirs." I did not question him as to why we were going. I got ready to go. He and I were the only two going. He told MSG Parker he was in charge and not to go on any operations until he returned. He instructed SFC Hoffman to stay in the compound and not to do any health and welfare work that day. He told them, "We will be back before dark." He told Sergeant Dot to enjoy a day off because he was driving, and away we went.

It was a fast trip. We arrived at the headquarters building with the air conditioners humming. This seemed to really set him off. When we walked into the headquarters, LT F said nothing to anyone. He went straight to LTC Speirs's door and, without knocking, turned, looked at me, and said, "Come on." He opened the door. LTC Speirs was behind his desk, drinking a cool-looking drink with

the glass filled with ice. LTC Speirs looked as if he was expecting LT
F. LT F said, "Let me see the fire support plans for that operation at
Gia Ray Mountain." LTC Speirs said, "I did not approve that operation." LT F then asked, "The team did not follow instructions and
let you know they were going on an operation in that area?" LTC
Speirs said, "I knew about the operation from the radio." LT F said,
"You let a green wet-behind-the-ears lieutenant go on an operation
in the hottest area in the province without a fire support plan? You
got them killed!" LTC Speirs yelled, "Get out of my office before I
have you arrested! I don't care if you are a hero!" LT F looked at him
and said, "LT R will be taking my team. It would be best if you don't
let anything happen to them."

The next week, MSG Parker called the province headquarters
and told them that LT F was taking the whole team to Saigon to see
him off and get a few days' rest. The response was, "You are good
to go. Have a good time. By the way, the operations officer wants
to speak to LT F." I heard the operations officer tell the others to
leave the room. LT F got on the radio and told us to clear out of the
command post or CP. They talked just for a few minutes, and LT F
came out and said, "That lying SOB," and that was all he said. MSG
Parker drove, and all five of us packed into our best jeep, which was
black, covered, and rode like a dream. You see, we were only authorized one jeep and a quarter-ton truck. The team had three jeeps,
two possibly stolen, and a VIP jeep, which was also maybe stolen.
Anyway, we were on our way to Saigon. It was a bittersweet trip. LT
F was leaving, and tonight would be our last party night with him.
We were going to make it a night to remember.

We arrived at the hotel. LT F had instructed me to bring my
class A or dress uniform. I did as I was instructed. By the time I
dressed, LT F was in his class A as well. The Silver Star stood out
like a signal: I was there, and I did my duty. The Big Red One patch
completed the picture. He told the other members to get started and
that he and LT R had some business to take care of. They said okay.
We left, and LT F drove us to MACV Headquarters. We went inside,

and I met a major I knew from Fort Polk. I introduced him to LT F. They seemed to get along right from the start. LT F said, "LT R, why don't you stay here with the major. I have some business upstairs." With that, he was gone. An hour later, LT F came back in and asked me if I was ready to go. I said, "Sure." He looked at the major and said, "Get good people for my MAT. I know where you live." With that, they both laughed.

LT F seemed happier than I had seen him in weeks. "Let's go party, LT R." Then he looked at me and said, "Take care of my team," for the last time. We left the headquarters and hooked up with the team in the hotel bar. That night, we must have gone into most of the dives in Saigon. Finally, LT F said, "I have had it!" He and I went back to the hotel. I was asleep by the time my head hit the pillow. The next day, LT F's "freedom bird" took him home. We stayed two more days, and then we headed back to our area of operation or AO, stopping by province headquarters on the way back. Another three days to remember. MSG Parker asked, "LT R, are we going to stop at P Headquarters?" That question hit me like a brick. It was the first time I knew I was now responsible for our MAT. I had been told time and time again by LT F that the team would be mine when he departed.

With MSG Parker's question, I realized I was in charge. I looked at the team and said, "I suppose we should stop and tell them we are back in town without LT F. That should make LTC Speirs happy." They all laughed and said, "Why not! Let's make his day!" We drove into province headquarters' parking lot at about 14:00 hours, and we all got out of the jeep.

SFC Hoffman said, "I will share some of the food and stuff we picked up this morning."

I said, "Okay by me. Just don't give them any of the good stuff." We all had a good laugh, and I went into the headquarters with MSG Parker.

We walked into the operations section, and MSG Parker said, "I will check and see what's been going on during our absence." As we walked further into the operations section, Captain Blankenship came up to us, and I noticed he was now Major Blankenship.

I looked at this oak leaf and said, "Congratulations."

He said, "Thanks," and then he asked, "How was the send-off for LT F?"

I told him, "We hit every sleazy bar in Saigon and had to be poured into bed. I managed to ensure LT F was poured into bed alone due to the fact, as he put it, he was going home to 'Mommy.' He told me if I let him get into trouble, I was a dead lieutenant."

Major Blankenship laughed and said, "Good show. I wish I could have been there."

I said, "We consider you part of our extended team, and you would have been welcomed." He said thanks, and I replied, "I guess I had better say hello to LTC Speirs."

MAJ Blankenship looked at me kind of funny and said, "You don't know?"

I said, "What don't I know?"

"LTC Speirs left the next day after your team went to Saigon."

"I thought he had months to go on his tour here."

MAJ Blankenship said, "He did, does. All I know is about ten hundred hours, the day after you guys left, he answered a call, and by fifteen hundred hours, he had cleared his desk and packed his bags, they were loaded up, and he was gone."

"What happened?"

"I thought you would tell me."

I said, "All I know is we stopped by MACV headquarters, I met an old friend from Fort Polk, LT F told me to tell my friend war stories, and then he went upstairs for about an hour. When he came back down, he called to me and said, 'It's party time,' and we were off."

MAJ Blankenship said, "That figures. LT F has some very powerful friends." I did not say anything, but I knew something had made LT F's day when he came back to get me. He had not been in a party mood before he went upstairs, but something had made him very happy. He said nothing, though, and I did not ask, of course.

MAJ Blankenship added, "The new LTC reported in yesterday, and his first instruction was for me to give him a status report on all the MATs, where they were, and what operations they were involved in. His name is LTC Silver, and he asks a lot of questions. After the review of all the MATs, he instructed me to inform them there would be no operations without his approval. He then called each commander and told them it was not his intent to hamper their initiative, but it was his intent that he be allowed to do his job. He also told them to have the balls to speak up when they thought something was not right. He then said he would be out to visit each team, and he was prepared to spend the night with them. You could just hear the relief in their voices. Change is here."

He continued, "By the way, when he made his way to your team, he said, 'When they get back, I want to see LT Robinson first. Then I want to meet his team. The team will be his until I can get a first lieutenant or captain to assist and replace him as team leader.' I don't know how he knew you were in Saigon, saying good-bye to LT F, but he knew. I guess it's time to meet your new boss."

With that, I followed MAJ Blankenship back to LTC Speirs's, now LTC Silver, office. The major knocked on the door, and a voice said, "Come in." We entered. The office had been rearranged—a couch, two chairs, and a coffee table had been added. He was seated behind his desk, but he stood on his feet and walked around his desk to shake my hand before I could even think about reporting to him. He told us to take a seat. We both sat on the couch. LTC Silver said, "I'm sure MAJ Blankenship has already told you about my conversations with the other MATs. Are there any questions?"

"No, sir."

"Good. I'm also sure he told you I plan to leave you in command of your team until I can get a first lieutenant or captain in here to replace you if that is possible. I understand you have a team that is very well put together. I know how loyal a group of men, especially soldiers, can become when they form bonds under the conditions your team operates. LT F (I could not help noting he called him LT F) has developed one of the best MATs in Vietnam. He has developed you to take his place. I have no problem with that, but the MATs require two officers for security and operational reasons. Two second lieutenants would be just too much 'gold' on one team." MAJ Blankenship and I got the joke at the same time. We laughed. He told the major, "You have to get faster on picking up on my jokes. You could be replaced by a second lieutenant, almost the same amount of gold as on the gold leaves." We then had another good laugh.

LTC Silver said, "I understand your team calls you LT R."

I said, "Yes, sir, when I can hear them."

"Good point!" Then he laughed. "MAJ B, I think I like that method of identification. Do you mind, MAJ Blankenship?"

"No, sir."

"Good. MAJ B, could you get us a cup of coffee, if that is okay with LT R?"

I said, "Coffee sounds good to me." MAJ B was up and gone like a bullet. He was gone just a few minutes, but before he could sit down, LTC Silver said, "MAJ B, could you give LT R and I a few minutes alone?" MAJ B said, "Sure," and left the room. LTC Silver said, "I have reviewed your team and the other teams' records. I will not be making many changes, but I expect to be involved not as a controller but more as a resource to assist you in getting your advising jobs done. We will operate as a team. You play on my team, and I play on your team. You know, I said earlier how close soldiers can become when they operate alone or in small groups and have to rely on their buddies or others to save their butts. I'm sure you noticed I'm not infantry. I'm a field artillery officer and have spent more time than I now like to think about as a forward observer here in Vietnam. I learned the importance of being able to rely on those who support you. My concept of operations is simple—you lead your team during their mission. I lead the province team, which includes your team, in doing the mission that we are assigned. I'm a strong believer in loyalty, and to be loyal, you have to have the balls to speak your mind. I expect it. In fact, I demand it. Do you have any questions about how I will command?"

"No, sir."

"Good. Now I would like to meet the rest of your team."

"Yes, sir." I started to get up, but he said, "Keep your seat." He went to the door and asked MAJ B if the MAT was ready to meet their new boss. I heard a number of "Yes, sir," and my MAT filed in. MSG Parker and the others, including Sergeant Dot, saluted, and in unison said, "MAT, best damn MAT in Vietnam, reporting as ordered."

LTC Silver returned their salute and said, "So I've heard. But the other teams told me while you all were in Saigon partying, they were here doing their job." The room became a little quiet. "Just kidding." We felt relieved. "I know you do your job well, and you are a very strong team. You are all to be congratulated. I know it's not easy out there. Sit down. I would like to talk to you about my command style. I have already discussed it with LT R, so I see no reason he should have to pretend to listen while I give you the same spiel." He then turned to me and said, "Why don't you go have a drink or something with MAJ Blankenship—I'm sorry, MAJ B." I stood to my feet and was out of the room. I heard LTC Silver say, "After I give you my spiel, I expect to hear from you. After we all have our say, I would like a few moments alone with each of you. I promise to give you time enough to get home (our compound) before dark." I closed the door, and MAJ Blankenship was waiting outside and said, "Let's go get a drink."

I said, "Sounds like a good idea to me." He turned to the office and, to no one in particular, said, "Tell LT R's team members we are at the snack bar and to join us there." We heard several okays, and we walked out the door and headed across the compound to the snack bar. No sooner had we sat down when MAJ B asked me again to level with him about LT F: "Who did he see? What went on?" I gave him the same answer as before: "Nothing. I was just keeping company with an officer I knew from Fort Polk."

MAJ B said, "Well, the day after you left, about ten hundred hours, LTC Speirs got a call, and all you could hear was, 'Yes, sir,' 'No, sir,' 'I understand, sir.' When he hung up the phone, he came out of the office in a rage. He told me to help him pack his gear because he would be leaving that afternoon, and his replacement would be here the first thing the next day. I asked him what was going on, but he looked at me and said, 'Don't pretend you don't know.' I didn't know. We packed him up, and the driver took him to Saigon, and that was the end of his command here. LTC Silver arrived, as LTC Speirs had said, the first thing the next morning. "LTC Silver gave us the same spiel he gave you, called all his subordinate units, introduced himself, and gave them the same spiel too. He has not stopped since he arrived. He has gone over all the operations for the last two years, talked to everyone on the staff, invited his Vietnamese counterparts to dinner, and, as you can see, is still going strong. He knows more about the province now than any of us. He has asked me a thousand questions about the Vietnamese commanders and the teams that advise them. Your team was no exception. He is going to be a very different commander than LTC Speirs. I expect he will be hands-on, hands-off kind of commander. He will do his job, and I expect you had better do yours. What do you think of him so far?"

I said, "I'm just getting used to my new role as team leader, but the first impression is he will be good to work for."

MAJ Blankenship said, "I think you are right. I know he told you he is going to leave you in command of your team until he gets a first lieutenant or captain."

"Yes, he did." Then SFC Brown (heavy weapons) and SFC Taylor (light infantry instructor), advisors on the team, came in and sat down at our table. Both of them said, "In our private talk with him, he wanted to know if we wanted off the MAT. We both said, "No. What's going on?" MAJ B said, "I think he has asked all team members that question. I think if you had said yes, he would have found you another assignment. He does not want anyone out there that doesn't want to be an advisor. I agree with him on that score." All of us chimed in with agreement. The other team members came in, and they all said they were asked the same question: "Do you want off the MAT?" Answer: "No." Sergeant Dot wanted to know why he would be asked. We explained what we thought the case was, and Sergeant Dot said, "I agree. If you don't like living with my people, they know it. We have a good team. All the PF and RF forces and the people in the villages like and respect our team. That is what I told LTC Silver. He is a different commander than LTC Speirs. He shook my hand and told me how much he appreciated my and my wife's work. How did he know about my wife?" No answer came from any of us. LTC Silver had done his homework. After all, Sergeant Dot's wife was the best cook in the province, and everyone knew it. We were very lucky to have both of them on our team.

After meeting LT Silver, we all loaded up, and away we went. CPT Knew was waiting for us with a dinner laid out in the village. He seemed glad to have us back. He said they went on a nighttime operation the night we left and ran into some local VC, but no big deal, no casualties on either side. I was glad. We had known most of the soldiers in CPT Knew's company. The next day, we went to a village near the Gia Ray Mountain to assist the local PF in building a protective barrier around their village. They needed razor wire and some other construction material to complete the project. The PF was made up of old men, young boys, wounded soldiers, and a few women from the village. They had accomplished very much with what they had. They had cleared fields of fire around their village and built some excellent firing positions. I was impressed with their work and asked the team if they wanted to spend the night there. Sergeant Dot said, "Let me ask the village chief." He came back in a few minutes and said, "The village chief would be honored to have us spend the night in their village."

We unloaded our equipment and gave the village chief the extra ammunition we had. The village chief was also the commander of the PF. Of course, after a hard day's work, with the team doing their share, it was time for the village to show their appreciation. What a dinner! They had everything from soup to nuts. It was one of the best dinners we ever had. Everyone was in high spirits. Of course, LTC Silver had said okay to our plan. He said he would lay on some fire support just in case. What a difference a colonel makes—he who wears the rank. You could tell he took his job to heart. That included providing us support. We took turns that night on radio watch. At around 01:00 hours, LTC Silver was on the phone asking for a status report. SFC Hoffman was on radio watch, and I was half-asleep. I saw no reason to get up. SFC Hoffman and he talked for a few minutes, and I heard SFC Hoffman say, "Out here."

The next morning, there was an engineer company a few miles from us working on the main road. I asked SFC Brown and SFC Taylor if they thought the engineers would have anything that they were willing to give us. Both said engineers always have stuff to give away. "Let's go get the village chief and see," SGT Dot said and went to get him, and when he came back all smiles, I knew it was okayed by the chief. We loaded up in our jeep, and away we went. The lieutenant in charge was glad to help. He loaded up a truck with materials to include some metal sheets used by temporary runways. They made excellent instant sidewalks. He asked if we could use a grader and operator for a few hours. Of course, we could! So back we went to the village, the lieutenant and his crew just behind us. The lieutenant said they were ahead of their timeframe, so he was glad to give his men something else to do. The village chief asked Sergeant Dot to find out how many engineers were working on the project. I was a little suspicious about the question. Sergeant Dot saw my worry and quickly added, "The village chief wants to prepare a meal for all of them." I laughed and told the engineer lieutenant what the village chief wanted to do. He said it sounded good to him.

The engineers, with their equipment, made more firing positions, dug connective trenches, dug outside latrines, laid some sidewalks, and by 13:00 hours, the village was a new place. The village people had been hard at work too. I could not help but notice and hear chickens being killed. At about 13:30, the village chief asked us to come and eat. The layout of food was beyond anything I had ever seen. The engineers pulled out their cameras out and were taking pictures. Most of them wanted their pictures taken with the beautiful young girls. They also wanted pictures with the village chief. The engineers came in shifts, but there was plenty of food for all of us. The lieutenant said, "If there is nothing else we can do, I guess I had better get back to the road project." The village, including the village chief, assembled to say good-bye. The rainy season was just beginning, so the sidewalk was a godsend to the locals. In the rainy season, without something to walk on, they could easily step up to their ankles in mud. No fun, and the mud, when dried, was like cement. What a good day in a land of war—from muddy shoes, and boots, to helping a village.

Chapter 11

Under LTC Silver's leadership, good things were happening in the province. The RF, and even the PF, was getting equipment and supplies that they had not been able to get beforehand. Either we were getting more money or the money was being used differently than it had been previously. All I know was the Vietnamese soldiers seemed to be getting paid, and a soldier who gets paid is a happy soldier. His voice said, *I know that you have been thinking about me, and that is good. I can assure you that I am always with you. Tonight, as you are almost asleep, I come to you to tell you that the days ahead will be filled with conflict for the way you are. From the time of your conception, I know how you would reflect the different aspects of who I am. As you go through the days and months ahead, just remember I am always with you. Now go to sleep. Your days are full. Just keep doing what your mind, soul, and heart tell you.* With these words, the warm embrace I had felt so many years ago when my cousin pulled me from the lake came over me, and I was asleep.

The next day, we received a call from MAJ Blankenship. MAJ B told us to move to help and train the PF and the village PF forces at Langue River. The move from Gia Ray Mountain to Langue River had been coordinated with the district team in that area, and they had been informed we would be moving. LT F had told me, "You, we, our team is not controlled by any district team. Our team works for the province, and we move a lot." This was our first move since LT F had left. We had gone to three or more villages before he left.

I asked MAJ B, "When do we move?" He said, "Today. You are a 'mobile' advisor team, aren't you?" He laughed. I said, "We will be on our way in an hour." MAJ B said, "Good. I will inform LTC Silver that you are on your way. By the way, the RF commander there is CPT Nguyen. I think you have met him before here at province headquarters." I had. He was older and had been a regular officer in the South Vietnam army before he was badly wounded. He still walked with a bad limp. I had liked him from the first time I met him. He had been gracious enough to show our team the town of Xuân Lôc. I guess what I liked most about him was when he took us to a Vietnamese restaurant and were served an excellent meal, I noticed he paid for the meal. Sometimes they did not, I learned from LT F. When that happened, he always left enough money on the table to cover for the meal. A meal like the one we had just consumed could place a real hardship on the owner. LT F had explained to other hosts that it was an American custom to leave money on the table after a good meal as a way of saying thank you. I followed his practice, and no one seemed to be offended. It worked, and the team always left some money. The word got around, and every place we went to eat, the service was excellent, and the food "for an American who liked their food" was outstanding.

The team had our gear loaded, and Sergeant Dot and his wife were ready to go within the hour. CPT Knew was there to see us off with several of his NCOs. We said our good-byes and told each other to be safe. I wondered how you do that in a war. I guess it is just anxiety among friends who know the danger each one faces. We arrived at Langue River at about 17:00 hours. The team house had been cleaned and vacated, and CPT Nguyen was there to welcome us to his command. MSG Parker had called province operations when we left, and he was now on the radio, reporting that we had just arrived without incident. I heard him say, "Yes, sir," and then he looked at me and said, "LTC Silver wants to talk to you."

He handed me the headset, and I said, "Sir, LT Robinson."

He said, "Get settled in and call me back at about twenty-two hundred hours." I said, "Roger." He said, "Roger and out." I handed the headset back to MSG Parker and, with a shrug, said, "Don't ask me." We unpacked and set up everything. The team house was a former central point for crossing the bridge. It had been reinforced. The courtyard was still there, but a bunker had been added. CPT Nguyen lived in one end of the compound, and most of his NCOs lived in different places around the team house, the bunker, and CPT Nguyen's quarters. It was a good spot. The original bridge had been blown up, and the middle section had fallen into the river. This section had been replaced with steel sheets, and because this was a major road between Saigon and I-Corps, the most northern part of Vietnam controlled by the Saigon government, it was one of the most important bridges and had to be protected at all costs. CPT Nguyen and his RF company were the men for the job. I wondered what was going on and why our MAT was there. At 22:00 hours, I was going to find out.

MSG Parker, SFC Brown, and SFC Taylor were going over the maps of the area. MSG Parker said, "We don't need to be blind if we have to get out of here." I agreed and was sorry I had not suggested that we do exactly what they were doing. We all sat down and studied the maps, and I thought of how much I relied upon MSG Parker. At 22:00, MSG Parker contacted province operations and told them I was standing by as instructed by LTC Silver. LTC Silver came on the radio and said, "LT Robinson, get CPT Nguyen. I want him to hear this also." SGT Dot went to get CPT Nguyen. LTC Silver said, "I know you and your team know how important this bridge is, so tonight we are going to enhance the protective fire plans for that bridge. I am sure CPT Nguyen's superiors have told him what we are planning to do. The reason I want him in the room is to get his input and, more importantly, make him part of the team that plans these supporting fires. It's going to be a long night for all of us."

Sergeant Dot came back into the room with CPT Nguyen, four of his officers, and two senior NCOs. I told CPT Nguyen that LTC Silver was on the speakerphone and would like to talk to all of us. CPT Nguyen nodded, and LTC Silver came on the speakerphone, greeted CPT Nguyen, and informed him that he had General Long, the senior Vietnamese officer, and Col. Street, an American senior advisor, in his office, and he had their support to fire the current fire support sites and then add to or change fire support sites upon our request. "What you will see and hear tonight is the fire support you would have received if your unit or the bridge had been attacked. You all know how critical this bridge is. At 23:00 hours, the fire support will come from both American and Vietnamese artillery units. In addition, naval gunships will also plan some supporting fire. Your job, CPT Nguyen and LT Robinson, is to have your commands observe, change, add to, or give us your best estimate of how effective these supporting fires would be. General Long would now like to say a few words."

Sergeant Dot said, "Yes, sir. I will interpret the general's remarks." The general again went over the importance of the bridge and thanked LTC Silver and us for our support. He then said that CPT Nguyen was the best officer for this important mission, and he said he was proud to have CPT Nguyen and his men under his command.

The show started at exactly 23:00 hours. Each fire support site was fired in turn. The sky lit up over the grid squares where the shells were exploding. We would mark the grid squares and discuss if that was the best location. The artillery firing went on for at least an hour. Then LTC Silver said, "It's time for the big guns." The Navy's big guns opened up on a grid square, the ground where we were actually shaking. This lasted only for a few minutes. Then LTC Silver asked if we wanted any changes made. We looked over avenues of approach, and there were three places that needed to be covered. CPT Nguyen and we agreed if we could add those three grids; they could cover any large force attacking the bridge.

CPT Nguyen asked me to propose, adding the grids to LTC Silver. I understood he did not want to appear to be critical of an old plan that the general had approved. I said okay, and I asked LTC Silver if the three sites could be added. He said, "Wait out." He came back in a few minutes and said, "Watch those sites." In about ten minutes, the sky lit up, and all three sites were being hit. You could tell by the look on CPT Nguyen's and his staff's faces they were pleased with the results. I informed LTC Silver we were in agreement with that kind of fire support, and CPT Nguyen felt certain he could protect the bridge. LTC Silver said, "We will number and hone the sites and send them to you. Good job to all of you, and the province wishes you all a good night's sleep. If there is nothing else. Good night." We all said, "Good night and out here." The fun was over. Radio watch started, and I took the first shift or watch.

The days at the bridge went quickly. We trained local RFs and PFs on some of the new stuff we had brought along with us. They loved the claymore mines. We demonstrated how to set them up and the safety procedures that needed to be followed. To ensure the point was driven home, SFC Taylor set up three of the claymores and tied them together with demolition cord. After putting an electric firing pin in a small amount of plastic explosives and connecting them all together, he took a copper wire, separated it from a battery with a plastic spoon, drilled a small hole in the handle, tied a trip wire to it, and then ran the wire across a trail. He then invited the RF company to walk down the trail. CPT Nguyen took several of his men down the trail, and as soon as they hit the trip wire, the claymore mines went off. Of course, SFC Taylor had made sure that CPT Nguyen and his men were not in the kill zone. He showed them what would have happened if they had been in the kill zone. The claymores had been positioned to kill anyone walking down that trail. They were eager and ready to learn this new method of using claymore mines.

We spent most of the time training, and I must admit most of the time was spent setting up ambushes using claymore mines. As I was to learn later, you could kill or maim a large number of soldiers or people or animals using this technique. I had started swimming in the river every day, along with the kids from the village. There was a steel cable that was strung across the river where the old bridge's concrete slabs had fallen into the river, and by holding onto the steel cable, you could get in between the two slabs, and it was like being in a washing machine, I guess. The river water would toss you up and down as it poured through the slabs. What fun. LTC Silver flew over one day and spotted me in the river, but all he said was to be careful.

That same week, an engineering company was having some kind of inspection, and a couple of trucks they didn't want inspected came to the river. The river was also a watering point to get water for road projects, so that was a good place to hang out. One of the drivers decided to go for a swim in his jungle fatigues. His pockets filled with water, and the current pulled him under. What a waste of a young life over an inspection in a combat zone without even being in combat. The local fishermen knew the river and had his body out on the sand in short order. The young kid, the soldier, looked at peace. We were at the team house when we heard the shouting. MSG Parker grabbed the radio, and we went to see if we could be of help, but we could not. I told MSG Parker to give province a situation report, a sit rep. He put MAJ Blankenship on the phone and informed him what had happened. LTC Silver called later that day and ordered me not to swim in that river again. All I could say was "Yes, sir. Roger out." The next morning, he called and said, "Go for a short swim, pack up your things, and head to Gia Ray Mountain. Let me know when you get there." I replied, "Yes, sir. Roger out."

I took him at his word and told MSG Parker to get our jeeps packed. We were headed back to the mountain. I took enough candy to feed an army and headed to the river for my last swim and to give the kids some farewell candy. There were only four or five kids there when I first arrived, but in just a few minutes, the banks and the river were full of kids. MSG Parker came down to get me, and of course, I was in the water. He said, "I thought LTC Silver ordered you to stay out of the river."

"He did, but this morning he said to go for a final swim." MSG Parker did not laugh often, but he laughed and said, "I work for a couple of nuts. Sir, we are ready to go." We pulled into our compound at 15:00 hours. CPT Knew was there to welcome us home, so to speak. We unpacked our gear, and CPT Knew said he would like to talk to me after we were settled. I said, "Roger that, sir." I always said "sir" to a higher-ranking officer. I did not care if they were not American. Some officers and enlisted men had a problem with showing proper respect to allied officers and senior NCOs. Thank goodness no one on our team had that problem. As a matter of course, the Vietnamese soldiers followed suit and showed us proper respect.

We finished unpacking, and I went to find CPT Knew. He was in his operations tent, going over some maps. He looked up and said, "Let me show you something. Intelligence has spotted (which meant someone reported) an NVA force in our area conducting recruitment efforts and collecting supplies, equipment, and money from the villages. I would like to set up ambushes here, here, and across this main infiltration route. What do you think?" He had it all planned out. I looked over the layout and asked him what the team could do to help. He said, "You know LT Short (not his real name, just what we called him because he was only four feet tall)?" I said, "Sure. He is an outstanding officer from what I can tell." CPT Knew said, "I agree. That's why I want him to lead the ambush along the main infiltration route. If province intel has it right, he should be able to handle the NVA force."

I had not noticed, but MSG Parker had come in as I was looking over the plan again. I turned to CPT Knew and said, "Do you think LT Short would mind if I went along with him and his soldiers?" CPT Knew smiled and said, "I don't think so." MSG Parker spoke up and said, "When is kickoff time for LT R and me?" I was glad that MSG Parker had volunteered, and so I did not have to pick one of the other team members. It was late, and we had to clear the operation with province, or so I thought. LTC Silver came on the phone as soon as we called them on the radio and said, "I know you and MSG Parker volunteered to go on this operation, and I approve of you taking part." It seemed he knew all along: news travels fast. "Our intel sources here and at MACV have confirmed there is an element of NVA terrorizing the local villages. Unchecked, that will undo all the good work that you and the team have accomplished in that area. Don't let this cloud your thinking. If CPT Knew has not told you, you know the village where your team and the engineers helped out?"

"Yes, sir."

"Well, the NVA killed the village chief last night." My God. He was only trying to make life better for the people living there. LTC Silver said, "I know fire support plans are in place for this operation. Air support has also been laid on just in case intel has the size of the force wrong." He said, "I'm glad to have soldiers like you and MSG Parker. You make me proud. Take care and don't hesitate to call for help. Out here. Roger out." The plan called for CPT Knew and another ambush group to leave first. Then LT Short's platoon, with MSG Parker and myself along to support if required, would leave last. LT Short spoke excellent English. In addition, his radio operator spoke good English. I decided Sergeant Dot would best be utilized in operations if we got into trouble. He could listen and pass information on to SFC Hoffman, SFC Taylor, and SFC Brown as to what was happening. They would then call for help. All this was in case LT Short and CPT French ran into a force they could not handle. LT Short and his squad leaders got their men into place. LT Short, MSG Parker, three of his soldiers, and I settled into our places.

The night was beautiful. The stars lit up the sky. There was only a sliver of moon, but you could see down the long path and among the rubber trees with the shadows playing tricks on your eyes. With a little imagination, you could see a whole army coming down that path. It seemed as if we had been there for hours, but in fact, we had been in position for only a couple of hours. This could be a long night. It was total silence. Two more hours passed, and then the shadows became real. The woods of rubber trees and the path were filled with NVA. Intel had it wrong. LT Short gave the order, and all hell broke loose. LT Short was badly hit in the arm. He asked me to take part of his platoon and cut off the NVA from flanking our position. MSG Parker was already on the phone, calling for fire support. LT

Short gave orders to a couple of his squad leaders, and he said, "They will follow you." With that, I said, "Theo, *tôi*" (Follow me.)

The NVA and our two squads were in a contest. If they won, they would flank LT Short's position and be able to bring killing fire on CPT French's position. The green tracers from NVA rifles were like the fireworks on the Fourth of July lighting up the sky. The NVA was putting down a heavy field of fire. We in turn were holding our own. Again all hell broke loose; our supporting fire was coming in. I don't know for sure who was adjusting fire, but it seemed like it was only a few feet away. The ground shook. In this case, the closer, the better. It seemed that the artillery fire lasted only a minute, and then it was over. Then the helicopter gunships were blasting away at positions provided to them by MSG Parker. We were still getting fire from the NVA, but the tide had turned. LT Short, with his arm bleeding badly, came up to me with his squad and said, "Let's go get the bastards," and with a yell, away we went toward what had been NVA positions.

We still were in the path when the NVA returned limited fire, but the firefight was over. We had won the fight. MSG Parker came up to me and said, "Sir, I will go into combat with you any day. You got balls!" I really did not know what he was talking about. The next day, CPT French and SFC Larson had cleaned and dressed LT Short's wounds. SFC Larson said if the bullet had been over just a little, he would have lost his arm. They came up to me, and both of them shook my hand. I asked what was going on. LT Short said, "If you had not led the charge, the NVA would have flanked our position, and the outcome would have been a disaster for us." I said, "Your men did that. Let's go buy them a bowl of soup. I'm hungry." When we walked into the cafe, the soldiers all stood up and gave us a hearty salute. CPT French said, "Carry on," and the talking began. CPT French and LT Short said, "You know they are talking about you." All I could say was, "You have to be kidding." I told the owner the soup was on me, and then I asked LT Short to translate for me. I made a short speech about how proud I was and how honored I was to serve with such brave men as CPT French, LT Short, and most importantly, "all of the soldiers like you. Now let's eat our good Vietnamese soup, the best in Vietnam!"

They all gave a good cheer, and we ate our soup. LTC Silver called later in the day. He was pleased, it seemed, that at least ten NVA soldiers had been killed or wounded, and they had two Chieu Hois, and not one of our soldiers had been killed. Several had been wounded but not killed. He said, "I understand you are a true infantry soldier now." I laughed and said, "Now you don't have to look the other way or back up when you pin on my combat infantry badge (CIB)." He laughed and said, "I will be glad to pin it on. I want to see you in a couple of days. I can't get time to come out there, so I guess it is about time for you and your team to go into Saigon, make your rounds, and stop by here on your way back to the mountain and see me. Any questions?"

"No, sir."

"Good. Out here."

"Roger. Out here."

The team left early the next morning for Saigon and our new piggy run. Boy, did we have a good run. The night clubbing and the great night in the hotel were a needed break for all of us. The mess hall gave us more good food than we had ever collected. We were going to eat well for the next month. We had our rest and a successful food run, and so we headed back to province. LTC Silver was waiting, or so it seemed; it always seemed as if he was waiting to see you. He told MSG Parker and me to come in and sit down. There was a major in his office, whom I recognized as the district team leader, just a few miles from province headquarters. LTC Silver said, "I believe you all know each other."

"Yes, sir," we all said.

"I have decided your team could, would be more effective if your team was located nearer province headquarters. Therefore, I have asked Major Butler if he can make room at his compound for your team. He has agreed. Your move will allow us to coordinate and plan actions throughout the province. I think your team has established the credibility to assist and advise any village, regional force (RF), or popular force (PF) in the province. I have run this plan through the Vietnamese chain of command, and they are in full support. But before I finalize this plan, I want your input." MSG Parker and I both gave our instant thumbs-up. This move would give us a seat or say in the planning of operations, and we could build a good team house. Of course, living well was not our first concern—okay, it ranks up there.

LTC Silver said, "With your support, I will brief the plan to MACV, and if all goes as planned, you guys can start work on your new team house next week." He was not fooled by our support, but it was nice. He knew and asked our input before he just told us what was up. Of course, MACV approved his plan, and we started work on our team house. CPT Knew even loaned us a couple of his soldiers to help. We had a good supply of water, so the first thing we completed was a shower. Of course, we could not say no when our Vietnamese soldier buddies came over asking to take a shower. We were the most popular team in Vietnam, or at least our shower was. The district team only allowed their team members to use their facilities. I could understand their reasons. They were a much larger team than we were. They left us to our business, and we did not interfere with theirs.

After the first week, we had moved in, but we were still changing and making improvements on our team house when we got a call from MAJ B that we were required at province headquarters the next morning at nine o'clock. This was not a problem; it was only a thirty-minute ride. The team loaded up and reported as ordered.

Chapter 12

The new team house was working out fine. A new lieutenant had been assigned to the MAT, and this one seemed to be able to work with the Vietnamese without them getting upset. The first lieutenant assigned after LT F left and was temporarily in charge of the team only lasted less than a month, and then I was back in charge as team leader. I learned later that the Vietnamese chain of command had asked that he be replaced.

At the team house, we were told that the Province Exchange System or PES needed someone with the expertise to be in charge. He was an accountant, so he seemed to fit. But I also wondered if it was because he was black. The team liked him, and he was happy to go to province. Of course, that gave our team an "in" at the PES, and he would and could get us anything we wanted. I guess everything works out for the best. We went another month with just one officer on the team: me. Then another second lieutenant arrived, LT Lyon. He was working out. He had very blond hair, and the kids loved to rub his head. They would laugh, and he did not seem to mind the attention. I think the way to the hearts of people is through their children. It seemed to be working for us.

We hit the road, going all over the province, assisting villagers in beefing up their security systems, improving their compounds, and as always, SFC Hoffman came to improve their health practices. SFC Brown and SFC Taylor were kept busy showing the local PF and RF how to set up daisy chain ambushes using explosives, DET cord, and claymore mines. I kept my fingers crossed we would not have a serious accident. If not set up and taken down properly, someone was going to get killed or hurt. So far, our luck was holding. Both SFC Brown and SFC Taylor had managed to stress the importance of safety. The local farmers and villagers woke up early to go to work in the fields, so any ambush had to be dismantled early, or you could potentially kill a whole family. This had happened in one of the other provinces. We did not want it to happen in ours.

One morning, we received a call early to go to a village near Gia Ray Mountain. It seemed the local PF had set up a daisy chain ambush and killed and wounded several NVA soldiers. It was uncommon for a PF unit to be so successful. We loaded up with extra supplies, and away we went. The carnage was awful, even if they were NVA. It was hard to tell for sure how many had been killed at first glance. The explosion had torn bodies apart. CPT French was there with his RF unit. He was in the process of recording the number of casualties and communicating with headquarters. It was important and was stressed that the higher ranks in both American and Vietnamese headquarters needed a body count of those killed or wounded. MSG Parker received his numbers from CPT French, and French reported the same numbers to MAJ B at Province. There were no wounded. We provided the village with the supplies we had brought and, of course, replaced the claymore mines.

As I looked at the faces of the killed soldiers, I saw they all looked so young. What a waste war was. The very future of a country was now lying dead in the hot sun. A senior official, a colonel, arrived from somewhere. I had not seen him at the province before. He and his staff took several pictures, he handed the village chief a large envelope, and away they went. Even though this was a far more successful operation than the one under LTC Speirs, neither LTC Silver nor the province's bigwigs showed up themselves. CPT French said he and his company would stay for a few days and asked us to stay. MSG Parker called province and relayed the request. LTC Silver came on the radio, and MSG Parker handed me the headset. LTC Silver said it was a good idea, and he would lie on fire support just in case something happened. The second night, we used the fire support he had planned.

The NVA came back. It was a short exchange, and intel sources said the NVA unit had left the area. We went back to our team house. A shower—you don't miss anything until you don't have it. Then it becomes the most important thing in your day. A shower—with plenty of water. The team kept advising and going to operations—some hot, some not; just a day's work. I was in my eighth month and was leaving for R&R in Sidney, Australia, the next week. No operations, just a run to Saigon and the American base camps to replenish our food supplies. The willingness of their mess hall staff to give us food always made me feel good. Americans are, overall, a generous people. I wondered how many other units hit them up for food also. They always seemed to have something to share.

I flew to Australia the next Monday. It was a good flight. The Aussies were nice and showed us a good time. They had some support units in Vietnam, and the papers were filled with the price we the Americans and also the Vietnamese were paying in blood for that war. The papers also contained stories of the protests going on in the United States. The Aussies wanted to know how much longer we would be there. They remembered the French occupation. Was this war costing too much to continue? The political price was getting high, and they felt that this price, not the cost in money or lives, would have to be settled. I did not know enough to discuss it, but I knew if the political price became too high, we would, in fact, find a way out of it.

My week went by in a flash, and I was back in Vietnam. MSG Parker picked me up at the airport with LT Lyon, whom we still called the newbie. He was all excited to tell me about the firefight at Gia Ray Mountain. I had told him not to get the natives upset if they went to a unit around the mountain. They had gone, and it was a good fight. CPT French had a wounded shoulder, and LT Lyon had a small cut on his right ear. It was his badge of honor and a combat infantry badge or CIB action to boot. I was proud for him. In some units, he would have received a Purple Heart, but to his credit, he said he cut himself on some barbed wire. I wonder if he appreciated how close he came to having his blond hair split in the middle and his head with a nice hole through it. The thought made me almost sick. He had become a valuable member of the team.

The following week, SFC Hoffman received a message from home. One of his kids had a serious life-threatening type of cancer. Even before calling LTC Silver, I called my buddy in Saigon and told him the story. This was SFC Hoffman's third tour to Vietnam. He had paid his dues. My buddy said, "Have him here Friday. He will leave on a smoker Friday afternoon. Bring his equipment. I will have him cleared here. Did you clear this with LTC Silver?" I had to say, "No." He said, "Call him and give him the facts. Tell him I will have you a replacement Friday afternoon. See what buddies in combat can do for their fellow soldiers?" I called LTC Silver and filled him in. He said, "Good job, LT. In the future, call me before you lay on something like this." I said, "Yes, sir." He laughed and said, "I know this won't hamper you doing what's best for your team. Get SFC Hoffman packed. I will have someone here clear him. Your team has my permission to take him to Saigon tomorrow. Spend one night in Saigon and then get back here. I have work for you to do next week. See if your buddy will let you bring back your new medic." "Yes, sir." With that, he said, "Out here." "Out here, sir."

I went to tell the team the news. SFC Hoffman said, "How did you pull that off so fast?" I said, "It was not me but a team effort. Everyone knows you need to be home. Get packed, you and the rest of our motley crew. We get to have a night of partying in Saigon to send SFC Hoffman off to his home." Even though we hated to see him leave, the send-off made it bearable. LTC Silver knew how to lead, so he knew the send-off party would help. It did. We all felt like someone cared. We had a good night, and the next day, after getting SFC Hoffman cleared, ticket in hand, and loaded on a freedom bird, we went to MACV to thank my buddy. He said, "I guess everything went as planned." I said, "Yes," and handed him the bottle of cognac our buddy at the PES had found for us. This was the stuff that only the big shots could afford, even in Vietnam.

My buddy at first did not want to take it, but I said, "If you don't, I will have the team set you up in an ambush." He laughed and grabbed the bottle. He then said, "Let's go meet your new medic. By the way, he is a heavy hitter. He worked in all the big hospitals in the states, and according to his records, he can outperform some doctors I know." We both agreed and laughed. Our new medic was drinking coffee in the snack bar when we walked in. He rose to his feet and said without introduction, "I'm MSG Lyon." Turning to me, he said, "I understand I will be on your team as the medic." I said, "Yes, welcome aboard." He continued, "I understand you had an emergency, and your last medic had to leave on short notice." I said yes and explained why SFC Hoffman had to go home on such short notice. He said, "I volunteered for this assignment when I heard." My buddy shook his head in agreement. "My last number of years have been in hospitals. It will be good to be back with soldiers again. I am packed and ready to go."

MSG Parker had come in and had heard the exchange. He also welcomed MSG Lyon, and they picked up his belongings and went out to the waiting jeeps. MSG Parker put MSG Lyon's stuff in the trailer behind the covered black jeep and indicated that MSG Lyon should ride with us. MSG Lyon said, "Do all teams have one of these?" indicating the jeep. MSG Parker said, "Only if they stole it." We all laughed. We stopped by province headquarters and introduced MSG Lyon around. LTC Silver asked MSG Parker, MSG Lyon, and me to come into his office. We entered, and he said, "Sit." We did. He welcomed MSG Lyon to the province and told him he was joining one of the best teams in Vietnam. MSG Lyon said, "So I've been informed." LTC Silver then said, "I'm also aware of your skills as a medic, but there is another role that you have to fulfill, and that's a combat soldier, not like a combat soldier but a combat soldier. Do you understand that added responsibility, MSG Lyon?" He said, "I understand the duties. I'm not sure how proficient I will be in that role. It is a role I have not done. I have always worked in clinics and as a senior medic in hospitals. I'm willing to give it all I got."

LTC Silver looked at us and said, "I don't see how we can ask for any more than that. I want your team with CPT French's RF at Gia Ray Mountain the first thing tomorrow morning. Intel has a huge NVA force in that area. You will be there to assist an American and Vietnamese battalion in their operation as a blocking force. This province headquarters and Saigon do not want this NVA force to go past the mountain without paying a heavy price. The American unit has laid on the fire support plan, and I have reviewed it. You, they will have all the fire support from both air and heavy guns they need to suppress any type of NVA force."

I said, "Sir, wouldn't it be a good idea for us to get to the mountain tonight? We have all our weapons, including our two fifty-caliber machine guns with us. Our team never travels without our weapons." The colonel called for MAJ B and said, "LT R wants to take his team to the mountain this afternoon. Lay it on." He then turned to me and said, "That's a good idea. If you have no questions, I will let you be on your way. LT R, remember, the mountain is a major NVA infiltration route. Be careful."

How do you stay careful in a war? Keep your mouth shut. We left for the mountain after we were dismissed. I informed the team about the mission and what intel had said about an NVA force coming through infiltration routes. We were all glad to get to the mountain that afternoon so that we could get set up. The next morning came early. CPT French's unit was preparing for the NVA forces by laying down another ring of razor wire around the compound and carrying boxes of ammo to the three corners of the area. Something was up. We found CPT French giving orders to his troops, and everyone was in a rush. He asked us if we had any extra claymore mines. Of course, we did. He asked for them, and I said okay. He turned to one of the lieutenants, and in about two minutes, I could see the claymores were being placed so that anyone coming toward the compound would be blown to bits. CPT French turned to the team and said, "We may be in for a hot one."

He was right. At about 10:00 hours, the first APCs and tanks came roaring past our compound and through our small peaceful village. We stood on the berm and watched as they were roaring past. The noise was deafening because the road was just one hundred yards or so from our compound. The first APCs armored personnel carriers or tanks were about a quarter of a mile down the road when all hell broke loose. The NVA was attacking the lead American element from both sides. The APCs deployed in the wide open spaces on either side of the road that had been cleared of trees by bulldozers equipped with blades called Rome plows. The points on the blades split huge teak, mahogany, and other large trees as if they were small saplings. Then when vegetation grew on the cleared sides of the roads, they were sprayed with Agent Orange, a defoliant that killed or made the tree cover very light. There was no ambush in this area without being seen, but the NVA had set up with their weapons just inside the wood line.

From our vantage point, you could see the tracers and hear the shells and APCs explode. We received a request through province operations to secure a medivac zone for the wounded. CPT French received the same order from his superiors. We opened our front gates and set up and marked a landing zone between our compound and the road. The first APC with wounded came in before we had finished. MSG Lyon went to work. The APC unloaded the wounded and the first dead soldiers. The medivac chopper loaded at the same time another APC arrived with more wounded and dead. No time to think, just act. We loaded the wounded and dead on the choppers. Then we stopped loading the dead—there were too many. It was hell.

This went on all day with a few slowdowns in the combat. It was about 16:00 hours and a lull in the fighting when the tanks and APC started heading back toward Xuân Lôc or province headquarters. What the hell were we supposed to do? Two battalions of mechanized infantry, and they surely had not defeated the NVA, but they were leaving? If the NVA wanted to kill us, we would be dead in an hour. We were on pins and needles all night; no one slept. MSG Lyon said, "I did not sign up for this!" We all gave a nervous laugh and said, "Join the club."

Morning could not have come too soon. It seemed all quiet outside our compound. At Province, LTC Silver called and said, "The higher headquarters was concerned that the NVA would overrun the province capitol, and Saigon was not willing to take that chance, so you guys were left out in the bushes. It was believed you were too small a target for the NVA to take you on." I said, "Sir, that's the first time in my life that I'm proud to be unimportant!" We both had a good laugh. Then he said, "Intel thinks the NVA may have cleared out." I hoped so. He and intel were wrong.

The next morning, tanks and APCs came running down the road, in the same spot as the NVA attacked again. It was another day of hell. The young soldiers, both Vietnamese and Americans, were paying a high price; it was getting harder to understand as I helped MSG Lyon and became a hand-holder for some of the seriously wounded. It seemed like that helped. The day ended, and again there was a repeat of the day before, but the next day, they did not come back. Intel said the NVA had left the area. Good for the Intel boys. We went back to our home about noon, but before we left, we went to the village to say good-bye, and we had that outstanding Vietnamese soup. War went on. We were numb.

The day-to-day activities did not change. We were trained, and we went on operations. We did what soldiers do—sometimes with success, sometimes not so successful, but the team had not lost a member. However, I was getting short. I realized I had changed, but I did not know how much. Time would let me have glances of my old self, but those were fleeting. The team gave me a send-off much like we had given LT F. The team would be led by a senior captain from province. He was a good officer, and the team liked and respected him. They were in good hands. LTC Silver told me he had not known many officers that performed as well as I had. He was proud to be my commander. I told him how much I appreciated his leadership and support.

As I started to salute him, he came around his desk, gave me a big hug, and said, "Get out of here and enjoy your last night in Saigon with your team." I followed his example and the next day embraced each member of the team. It was a mixture of sadness and happiness as we parted ways. I gave MSG Parker a last hug and thanked him for his support and leadership. Then I was walking toward the freedom bird. I did not look back. If I had, I would have stayed. It's hard to leave one's family.

Chapter 13

Our freedom bird landed at Travis AFB, California, just before lunch California time. They had served us a steak meal just an hour or so before landing. No one needed to eat. The welcome crew did not ask if we were hungry. We were herded off the plane and into a large room. On the way into it, we saw a plane-load of newbies headed out. They were all smiles, joking and hitting each other on parts of each other's bodies that got them the most laughs. They were happy and having fun. There were also a few old-timers in the group returning to Vietnam. They were sober and knew the hell they could expect. I wondered how many of the youngsters would come back in a body bag and how many would be laughing and cutting up like they were doing today, when or if they returned. I knew the answer: none.

In our group, it had been a sober and quiet flight from Vietnam home. The young LTC came into the room and welcomed us home. Then he turned the processing over to a captain and an MSG, who then said the buses outside were marked with our airlines' destinations on them. "Please get on the bus marked with your destination airline," he said. "Is there anyone here who does not have an airline ticket or a way home or to your next duty station?" No one said anything. The captain looked pleased. "Those of you who are being picked up here, please go through the welcome rear door. Your rides home and the people taking you are in the lounge just outside the door. The rest of you, please secure your belongings and get on your destination buses. The buses will drop you off at the airlines. Arrangements have been made for you so that you do not have to process through lines in the airport to get on your planes. A representative from the airline will meet you and assist you on board. Again, welcome home and have a safe flight or trip to your next destination. Are there any questions?" No. "Good. Please get on the buses."

The bus ride to San Francisco airport was again quiet, and some of us slept. Just like the captain promised, I was met by a Delta Airlines representative or rep and was loaded on the flight without fanfare. I asked the Delta rep why the assistance. He looked at me and said, "Not everyone will welcome you home. It cuts down on the time needed to get our planes airborne and on schedule if we can keep the protests and conflict to a minimum. You will see what I mean in a few days." With that, he said, "You are free to board. Have a pleasant flight to Atlanta, Georgia." I had a window seat, and as the passengers were loaded, an elderly lady was shown the middle seat next to me. She looked at me and said, "This is my first flight, young man, and if I seem a little nervous, I am." We both laughed. I said, "I may sleep most of the way. Looking out the window at the clouds and the lights, if we get to Atlanta after dark, is worth half the trip." Since this was her first flight, I asked her, "Would you like to change seats with me?" She said, "Do you mind?" I said, "No. I just request one thing. If I start having a bad dream, you just punch me." She said she would, so we changed seats.

Then a young man my age sat down in the aisle seat. He looked at me with my tanned body and bleached-out hair and said nothing. The lady said to both of us, "I'm going to see my sister in Atlanta after thirty years, and this young man has given me his window seat, and I'm sitting with two of the best-looking men on this plane. It's going to be a good trip for me." The man in the aisle seat said nothing. I said, "I bet your sister is waiting for you with much joy in her heart, and I'm sure she has cooked the best Southern meal you have ever eaten. Don't gain too much weight." We both laughed.

The plane was taxiing down the runway for the takeoff. The smile on my window-seated lady was worth the switch. As the plane engines provided the thrust and the G-force held us slightly against the back of our seats, she grabbed and held my hand. I said, "That's a lot of power." By that time, the plane was airborne, and she relaxed. I said, "Please don't forget to punch me hard if I start having a bad dream." She made a fist and said, "Don't worry. I raised four boys, and I know how to use my fists." We laughed again. By this time, the aisle seat member of our group was looking around to change seats. He stood up and went to the back of the plane for another seat. The lady said, "I hope we did not upset him with our talking." I said, "I don't think that's why he changed seats. I think he didn't like my tan." She said, "What about my brown skin?" I said, "I doubt it. But regardless, it's his problem, not ours." She said, "You're right," and we both laughed.

The attendants came through the plane offering drinks and peanuts. I did not want any, but my new "window buddy" did, so she got orange juice, and I said, "I will also take an orange juice." As the stewardess went on down the aisle, I drank my OJ and told my "window buddy" I was going to sleep if she did not mind. She said, "Sweet dreams," and smiled. I was asleep in just a few minutes. I was back in Vietnam. It was an ambush, and the bodies were around me. Then I felt the hit on my side. I was on the plane home. My side had not been blown away but just given a good lick from my "window buddy." I looked at her and said, "Thank you." She said, "You're welcome."

I stayed awake the rest of the way to Atlanta. The lights were just coming on when we landed in Atlanta, and the wonder on my "window buddy's" face was something to behold. I recalled the first time I saw the skyline at night and my wonder at the lights. They were quite a show the first time. We taxied to our gate, and I helped my seatmate get her luggage down, and since I only had one small carry-on, I offered to carry one of hers. She said, "You're too kind." I said, "It would be my pleasure." We walked down the corridor, and her sister and a large group of her family members were waiting. She took the bag I was carrying and motioned for a young man to get it. Then she said to her family, "Meet my new friend," hugged me, gave me a big kiss, and said, "Welcome home." I shook hands all around and then saw my family members waiting for me. I said, "It was my pleasure flying with you," and then I went to be greeted by my family members. I found my bag, and we headed for the car.

The welcome I received from my "window buddy" was better than I received from my family. Oh well, things change. The next week, I called infantry branch and requested Fork Polk, Louisiana, versus Fort Stewart, Georgia, and they said, "Okay, you can go to Fort Polk, Louisiana, and if you want to report in early, that's okay too. We understand the home fires may not be as welcoming as you expected. It just takes time. So if you want to report in early, go ahead." I thanked the assignment officer for allowing me the flexibility. He said, "No problem." I was scheduled for a thirty-day leave but decided to report to Fort Polk early. I took less than two weeks off. Infantry Branch was right—I was uncomfortable at home. No one wanted me around, or so it seemed. If someone I had not seen in years asked, "Where have you been, and what have you been doing?" as soon as I said, "I'm in the Army," they looked at me kind of funny, and then when I added, "I just returned from Vietnam," that was the end of the conversation. It seemed no one wanted me around. I guess the "baby killer" thing applied to us all.

The antiwar movement was going full blast. It seemed the only place to go was the safety and acceptance of the Army. So, short of two week's leave, I was off to Fort Polk, my home. I arrived at Fort Polk, reported in, and was told I was to be the new commander of the Special Training Company or STC. I was glad to be a commander, but I asked the LTC who had just informed me of my new job, "Don't I have to be interviewed first?" He said, "Your new boss, the commander, reviewed files last week and told me that you were his selectee and to hell with the personal interview. You'll like him. He is direct, to the point, and gets the job done. He thinks you are the man for the job. By the way, if you are not up to it, he will fire you. The STC is a hard company to command. I will let your new boss fill you in. Do you need any assistance in getting settled in?"

"No, sir."

"Good. Then that's all I have for you. I know you have been stationed here before. Do you know where STC is and where the command building is?"

"Yes, sir."

"Good. I will inform your new commander you are on your way."

My new commander was waiting for me as soon as I opened the door to the command building. A voice said, "Get in here, Captain Robinson." I walked to his door and knocked, and he said, "Get in here." I did as I was told and reported in the best I could while he was walking around me, checking me out. He said, "I'm glad you are not a 'fatty.' Got a good haircut and don't have a mustache. Can't stand them." He then went back to his desk and picked up a fishing lure. He said nothing as he tied and retied the lure. It seemed like an hour. Then he said, "I picked you to command STC because I think you can handle it. Do you know the mission of STC?"

I said, "No, sir."

"Well, let me put it into a nutshell for you. You were a training officer here for a short time (he had done his homework by looking at my records). Those soldiers that were hurt are overweight, underweight, or just could not keep up with their peer group are often sent to STC for special training. That's one group. Another group is what is called the President and Secretary of the Defense's McNamara's 100,000. These soldiers have educational deficiencies that need to be corrected before they start in BCT. You will always have these two groups. The average strength of your company will be two hundred to two-hundred-fifty soldiers, sometimes more, all needing special attention. To accomplish this, you have at least five lieutenants and a noncommissioned officer assigned for every twenty soldiers. This does not include your special staff of cooks, bodybuilders, two clinical psychologists who were not officers, a chaplain on call at all times, and of course, a first sergeant. The current commander will be leaving next week. This gives you enough time to learn the ropes and get checked in with the cadre. That's about it from my side of the desk. Do you have any questions or need any assistance in getting settled in?"

"No, sir."

"Good. I will see you in the morning with the old commander in your mess hall." He roared out the door, "Has the old commander arrived yet?" A captain was standing in the door. "Old commander, meet the new commander. Now both of you get out of my office and go do what captains do." With that, I saluted and left his office, as instructed, with the "old commander."

As soon as we left the building, I said, "He said he would join us for breakfast tomorrow." "Yes, I heard him. By the way, he is the best commander I have ever worked for. Do your job, and he will support you one hundred and ten percent. He does not back down. This is the hardest and best job a captain can have. He told me last week that he had picked my replacement and that you would make me look like a babe in the woods. I'm not kidding. He is the best."

Over the next week, I met and talked to the company staff. It seemed most, if not all, of them were handpicked for the assignment to STC. The lower enlisted trainers were exceptional. They ran a physical training program for over a hundred soldiers and kept records on all of those soldiers in the convalescent platoon without fail. What a joy it was to see those young soldiers watch as their bodies changed into ones of strength and health. The bodybuilders knew their stuff. One of the psychologists and his wife became my own support in addition to supporting the assigned soldiers. I was adjusting to the changes that were occurring in my life. The Vietnam War had done something to my head. His wife was a very supportive influence when it came to her husband's work and could always say just the right thing at the right time to diffuse my bad moods. If the other lieutenants, or even the first sergeant, noticed anything wrong in my actions, nothing was ever said. The psychologist said I only let my true self show through to his wife. Their support was key in getting me through the first few months back home.

One of the duties I had was talking each week to every soldier. Sitting in on those talks would be either the first sergeant, their platoon sergeant, the chaplain, or one of the psychologists. The conversations went something like this: "Do you have any problems that we need to help you with?" "Is the food okay?" (Always important!) "Are you being treated fairly and with dignity and respect?" If the soldier had no problems or no complaints, notes were made on his counseling record, and he was allowed to rejoin his platoon. This activity took up several hours of my day. Some of these young soldiers, these kids, had some horror tales. Some had been both physically and mentally abused, some neglected to the point that they thought they did not have any worth, some had never heard the word *love* in reference to them—you name it. I was hearing some horror stories that made the year I had just been through seem like a walk in the park, or so it seemed. Events can screw your head up. His voice said, *You have been through a horrifying, dreadful experience, but the inner soul I gave you has not changed. You still care for and can relate to these soldiers better because of what you have been through. As I told you long ago, use your head and mind to do what is right for these men, and what you do for them you will do for yourself.* I smiled, and for a brief moment, I was at peace. This assignment, with his help, was going to be my salvation. It was.

The End

About the Author

The author grew up on a farm in rural Georgia and was the ninth child in a family of eleven. His parents impressed on their children the importance of self-reliance and self-respect. His mother often told them if you can't say something good about someone, don't say anything. His father stressed the importance of word and deed. Your word was your bond, and what you chose to say or do was your responsibility to stand up and take ownership for both! With these guide post, the author has lived out his youth and adult years.

CPSIA information can be obtained
at www.ICGtesting.com
Printed in the USA
LVHW09*2340180818
587420LV00002B/5/P